Playing
by the Rules

Playing by the Rules

A Basic Guide
to Interpreting the Bible

Robert H. Stein

Baker Books

A Division of Baker Book House Co.
Grand Rapids, Michigan 49516

© 1994 by Robert H. Stein

Published by Baker Books
a division of Baker Book House Company
P.O. Box 6287, Grand Rapids, Michigan 49516-6287

Printed in the United States of America

Library of Congress Cataloging-in-Publication Data

Stein, Robert H., 1935–
    Playing by the rules : a basic guide to interpreting the Bible / Robert H. Stein.
       p.   cm.
    Includes bibliographical references.
    ISBN 0-8010-8366-4
    1. Bible—Hermeneutics. I. Title.
BS476.S76   1994
220.6'01—dc20   93-44833

To

Steve and Liz

May the joys of your pilgrimage in life be
multiplied because they are shared, and
may the sorrows along the way be lessened
because they are borne together.

Contents

Preface

How can I justify writing a book on the study of the Bible when so many already exist? Both on the popular and the technical levels, there are numerous books on interpreting the Bible. How can I defend the publishing of still another? As a teacher I am well aware of the many books available on this subject. Many of them are well written. Yet for various reasons I believe there is a need for still another. This book is an attempt to present in a nontechnical way a text that will help the reader understand what the goal of reading the Bible should be and how this goal can be achieved.

In the first four chapters of this book I seek to demonstrate that the goal of reading the Bible is to understand what the biblical authors meant by their writings. Once this is understood, the next task is to discover the legitimate implications that flow out of this meaning, and how this applies today. To assist in this, I discuss and describe the roles that the author, the text, and the reader play in this process. A precise vocabulary is also provided in order to avoid confusion.

I then discuss the various kinds of literature found in the Bible. The description of a biblical text as being a proverb, a parable, a prophecy, or an epistle is of little value unless the "ground rules" governing these literary forms are understood. We know, for instance, that Luke 15:11–32 is a parable; Matthew 7:7–8 is a poetic form known as synonymous parallelism; and Jeremiah 4:23–26 is a prophecy. But what is the value of knowing this? How does this help us understand these passages? I have sought in this book to explain some of the rules that govern the interpretation of these various literary forms. How should prophecy be interpreted? Hyperbole? A biblical narrative?

The importance of interpreting the Bible correctly cannot be overemphasized. The claim that the Bible is inspired and that it is God's revelation to humanity is ultimately of little value without some understanding of how that divine revelation should be interpreted. When we describe the Bible as "infallible" or "without error," these terms are meaningless if we do not know how to interpret it. What do we mean when we say that the Bible is without error? What is it that is infallible? Is it my understanding of the Bible? Is it yours? Is it the particular translation of the Bible that I am using? Is it the Greek or Hebrew text that scholars use? Who gives meaning to a text? Can a text possess more than one meaning? Should we interpret the Psalms in the same way we interpret Romans? It is hoped that this work will provide the reader with answers to these and other questions.

The present work has been in process for nearly ten years. Much of it took shape in my teaching of a class called "Biblical Prolegomena," which has since been retitled "Hermeneutics." A great debt is owed to E. D. Hirsch, Jr. whose *Validity in Interpretation* has made a lasting impact on my thinking. Much of what is said in the opening chapters has been greatly influenced by him. This is especially true with respect to the vocabulary I use. I trust that my use of much of his vocabulary will be understood as a compliment rather than a theft! I apologize, however, for any ineptness that appears at times in my expression of similar views.

I wish to express my appreciation to my students for their assistance in understanding more clearly what is involved in the task of interpreting the Bible. To Duane Tweeten, Gary Johnson, and Michael Welch I want to express my appreciation for reading and critiquing an earlier form of this work. I want to thank Gloria Metz, the faculty secretary, whose assistance has made my task in writing this book much easier and more enjoyable. I am grateful for her assistance over the years in my various writing projects. She has truly been a "gift" during this time. I especially want to thank my colleagues, Arthur H. Lewis and Thomas R. Schreiner, for their many helpful comments. I would also like to express my appreciation to Wooddale Church of Eden Prairie, Minnesota, for its part in the publication of the present text. It was through my teaching a course on biblical interpretation in their lay school that the writing of the present work had its start.

Introduction

Tuesday night arrived. Dan and Charlene had invited several of their neighbors to a Bible study, and now they were wondering if anyone would come. Several people had agreed to come, but others had not committed themselves. At 8:00 P.M., beyond all their wildest hopes, everyone who had been invited arrived. After some introductions and neighborhood chit-chat, they all sat down in the living room. Dan explained that he and his wife would like to read through a book of the Bible and discuss the material with the group. He suggested that the book be a Gospel, and, since Mark was the shortest, he recommended it. Everyone agreed, although several said a bit nervously that they really did not know much about the Bible. Dan reassured them that this was all right, for no one present was a "theologian," and they would work together in trying to understand the Bible.

They then went around the room reading Mark 1:1–15 verse by verse. Because of some of the different translations used (the New International Version, the Revised Standard Version, the King James Version, and the Living Bible), Dan sought to reassure all present that although the wording of the various translations might be different, they all meant the same thing. After they finished reading the passage, each person was to think of a brief summary to describe what the passage meant. After thinking for a few minutes, they began to share their thoughts.

Sally was the first to speak. "What this passage means to me is that everyone needs to be baptized, and I believe that it should be by immersion." John responded, "That's not what I think it means. I think it means that everyone needs to be baptized by the Holy Spirit." Ralph said somewhat timidly, "I am not exactly sure what I should be doing. Should I try to understand what Jesus and John the Baptist meant, or what the passage means to me?" Dan told him that what was important was what the passage meant to him. Encouraged by this, Ralph replied, "Well, what it means to me is that when you really want to meet God you need to go out in the wilderness just as John the Baptist and Jesus did. Life is too busy and hectic. You have to get away and commune with nature. I have a friend who says that to experience God you have to go out in the woods and get in tune with the rocks."

It was Cory who brought the discussion to an abrupt halt. "The Holy Spirit has shown me," he said, "that this passage means that when a person is baptized in the name of Jesus the Holy Spirit will descend upon him like a dove. This is what is called the baptism of the Spirit." Jan replied meekly, "I don't think that's what the meaning is." Cory, however, reassured her that since the Holy Spirit had given him that meaning it must be correct. Jan did not respond to Cory, but it was obvious she did not agree with what he had said. Dan was uncomfortable about the way things were going and sought to resolve the situation. So he said, "Maybe what we are experiencing is an indication of the richness of the Bible. It can mean so many things!"

But does a text of the Bible mean many things? Can a text mean different, even contradictory things? Is there any control over the meaning of biblical texts? Is interpretation controlled by means of individual revelation given by the Holy Spirit? Do the words and grammar control the meaning of the text? If so, what text are we talking about? Is it a particular English translation such as the King James Version or the New International Version? Why not the New Revised Standard Version or the Living Bible? Or why not a German translation such as the Luther Bible? Or should it be the Greek, Hebrew, and Aramaic texts that best reflect what the original authors, such as Isaiah, Paul, and Luke, wrote? And what about the original authors? How are they related to the meaning of the text?

It is obvious that we cannot read the Bible for long before the question arises as to what the Bible "means" and who or what determines that meaning. Neither can we read the Bible without possessing some purpose in reading. In other words, using more technical terminology, everyone who reads the Bible does so with a "hermeneutical" theory in mind. The issue is not whether one has such a theory but whether one's "hermeneutics" is clear or unclear, adequate or inadequate, cor-

rect or incorrect. It is hoped that this book will help the reader understand what is involved in the interpretation of the Bible. It will seek to
do so by helping readers acquire an interpretative framework that will
help them understand better the meaning of biblical texts and how to
apply that meaning to their own life situation.

Part 1

The General Rules of Interpretation

1

Who Makes Up the Rules? An Introduction to Hermeneutics

The term "hermeneutics" frightens people. This is both unfortunate and unnecessary. The word comes from the Greek term *hermēneuein*, which means to explain or interpret. In the Bible it is used in John 1:42; 9:7; Hebrews 7:2; and Luke 24:27. In the Revised Standard Version the latter verse reads as follows: "And beginning with Moses and all the prophets, he [Jesus] *interpreted* to them in all the scriptures the things concerning himself." The New International Version reads, "And beginning with Moses and all the Prophets, he [Jesus] *explained* to them what was said in all the Scriptures concerning himself." The word translated "interpreted" and "explained" in these two versions of the Bible is the word [*di*]*hermēneuein*. A noun formed from this verb, *Hermes*, was the name given to the Greek god who was the spokesman or interpreter for the other gods. This is why in Acts 14:12 we read that after Paul healed a cripple at Lystra, the people thought that the gods had come to visit them. "Barnabas they called Zeus, and Paul they called *Hermes* because he was the chief speaker." (Cf. also Acts 9:36; 1 Cor. 12:10; 30; 14:5, 13, 26, 27, 28; etc.) The term "hermeneutics," which comes from these Greek words, simply describes the practice or discipline of interpretation. In interpreting the Bible, who determines the rules?

The Game Itself: The Various Components Involved in Hermeneutics

In all communication three distinct components must be present. If any one is lacking, communication is impossible. These three components are the *Author*, the *Text*, and the *Reader*, or, as linguists tend to

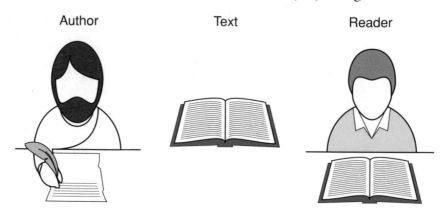

| Author | Text | Reader |

say, the *Encoder*, the *Code*, and the *Decoder*. Still another way of describing this is: the *Sender*, the *Message*, and the *Receiver*. (If we carry this over to the analogy of playing a game, we have the *Creator of the Game*; the *Game Parts* [pieces, cards, dice, board, etc.]; and the *Players*.) Unless all three elements are present, communication (the game) is impossible.

The main goal, or at least one of the main goals, of interpreting the Bible is to discover the "meaning" of the text being studied. We want to know what this text "means." Yet where does this meaning originate? Where does it come from? Some interpreters argue that it comes from one component, whereas others argue that it comes from another.

The Text (i.e., the Game Parts) as the Determiner of Meaning

Some have suggested that meaning is a property of the text. It is the text that determines what a writing means. We have probably all heard or even said something like, "Our text tells us . . . " And who has not heard Billy Graham say, "The Bible says . . . "? Yet those who argue that meaning is a property of the text mean something very different than what Billy Graham means. This view argues that a literary text is "autonomous." As a text it possesses semantic autonomy in the sense that its meaning is completely independent of what its author meant when he or she wrote. What the biblical author was thinking about and sought to convey by the text is quite irrelevant with respect to the meaning of the text. This is because a text possesses autonomy and is totally independent of its author. As a result, reading a related work such as Galatians in order to help us understand what Paul meant when he wrote Romans makes little or no sense. We could just as well read Charles Dickens' *A Tale of Two Cities.* Furthermore, what Paul actually meant when he wrote Romans is no more valuable in determining the actual meaning of Romans than any other person's opinion. According to this view, the text is independent of and has no connection with its author. It possesses its own meaning(s).

For Billy Graham, as he preaches from Romans, "The Bible says" and "Paul means" are synonymous. For those who argue that the text possesses its own meaning, however, these two things are not in any way the same. Every text is an independent work of art that is to be interpreted independently of its author. According to this view, when a work becomes "literature" the normal rules of communication no longer apply; this piece of communication has been transformed into a work of "art." Because it is art, the original composer no longer possesses control of it; the art itself possesses its own meaning completely apart from its creator. If in some way Paul could appear before those who argue for the semantic autonomy of the text and say, "What I meant when I wrote this was . . . ," the response would essentially be, "What you say, Paul, is interesting but quite irrelevant." Paul's willed meaning of his text, what he sought to communicate in his writing, is no more authoritative than any other person's interpretation. Thus, it is illegitimate to place any authorial control over the meaning of a text. This is a very popular approach among literary critics.

Perhaps the biggest problem with this view, that the text itself is the determiner of meaning, involves what a "text" is and what "meaning" is. A written text is simply a collection of letters or symbols. Those symbols can vary. They can be English or Greek letters, Japanese symbols, or Egyptian hieroglyphics. They may proceed right to left, left to right, up or down. They can be written on papyrus, animal skins, stone, or metal. Yet both the letters and the material upon which they are written are inanimate objects. Meaning, on the other hand, is a product of reasoning and thought. It is something only people can do. Whereas a text can convey meaning, it cannot produce meaning, because it cannot think! Only the authors and readers of texts can think. Thus, whereas a text can convey meaning, the production of meaning can only come from either the author or the reader.

The Reader (i.e., the Player) as the Determiner of Meaning

Some interpreters claim that the meaning of a text is determined by the reader. (This "reader" is sometimes called the "implied reader," the "competent reader," the "intended reader," the "ideal reader," the "real reader.") The person who reads the text gives to it its meaning or "actualizes" it. This should not be confused with thinking that the reader learns-deciphers-discovers-ascertains the meaning the text possesses in and of itself (the view described above). Nor should it be confused with the view that the meaning is determined by what the author meant when he or she wrote the text (the view described below). On the contrary, this view maintains that the person who reads the text determines its meaning. Each individual as he or she reads the text creates the meaning!

According to this view (sometimes called "reception theory," "reception aesthetics," "reader-response criticism," etc.), if different readers come up with different meanings, this is simply due to the fact that a text permits the reader to discern multiple meanings. Thus, we can have Marxist, feminist, liberationist, egalitarian, evangelical, or Arminian "readings" or interpretations of a text. This view assumes that there are many legitimate meanings of a text, for each interpreter contributes his or her meaning to the text. The text functions somewhat like an inkblot into which the reader pours his or her own meaning. Sometimes, in popular usage, we hear an individual say something like, "What this biblical text means to me is . . . " or, "This passage may mean something different to you but for me it means . . . " As we shall see later, however, such statements are best understood as describing the many different applications (or implications) of the author's intended meaning.

The Author (i.e., the Creator of the Game) as the Determiner of Meaning

The more traditional approach to the study of the Bible has been to see the meaning as being controlled by the author. According to this view, the meaning of a text is what the author consciously intended to say by his text. Thus, the meaning of Romans is what Paul intended to communicate to his readers when he wrote his letter. This view argues that if Paul were alive and told us what he meant to convey in writing Romans, this would settle the issue. The text means what Paul just told us he meant. (This is why in seeking to understand Romans it is more helpful to read Galatians, which Paul also wrote, than to read Ernest Hemingway's *The Old Man and the Sea* or Homer's *Iliad*.) Similarly, the meaning of the Gospel of Luke is what Luke purposely willed to convey to Theophilus when he wrote.

This view argues that the Bible and other great works of literature are not to be treated as unique works of "art" possessing distinct rules supposedly appropriate only to art. On the contrary, they are to be interpreted in the same way that we interpret other forms of verbal communication. This is essentially the commonsense approach to communication. All normal conversation assumes that the goal of interpretation is to understand what the speaker or writer means by the words he or she is using. We cannot even argue against this view without at the same time agreeing with it, for we must seek to understand what writers mean by their words in order to engage in discussion with them. For instance, in your attempt to understand this paragraph are you not seeking to understand what I wanted to communicate by it?

This issue has been a major one in the 1980s and 1990s with respect to constitutional law. The basic issue at stake in the Supreme Court nomination hearings of Robert Bork and Clarence Thomas involved whether the meaning of the Constitution is determined by what the original framers of the Constitution meant when they penned these words (the author) or what the present judges think that the words of the Constitution mean apart from the original intent of its framers (the text or the reader). On the one side a Supreme Court judge has stated that the desire to follow the original intent of the framers of the Constitution is "Arrogance cloaked as humility" and that "it is arrogant to pretend that from our vantage we can gauge accurately the intent of the framers . . . to specific, contemporary questions." On the other hand, James Madison argued long ago that if "the sense in which the Constitution was accepted and ratified by the nation be not the guide in expounding it, there can be no security . . . for a faithful exercise of its power."

It has been argued that "literature" is to be interpreted differently from all other forms of written communication. In other written works, as well as in general communication, we are to seek the author's intended meaning, but when a work becomes "literature" it is no longer to be treated in this manner. Literature does not fall under the rules of written communication but of "art." As a result the author's willed intention, what he meant when he wrote, is to be rejected or ignored, and meaning is to be determined either by the text itself or by the interpreter.

But who determines what is "literature"? There is no rule, law, or consensus that can be used to determine what is literature and what is not. (If we say that a work of literature is one that has been acknowledged over a period of time, then there is no such thing as a twentieth-century work of literature. If we say, on the other hand, that a work becomes literature when it has gained great popularity, then Mickey Spillane is the greatest writer of literature in the world!) The very fact that the classification of a work as "literature" is quite arbitrary indicates that to interpret such a work differently from all other written forms of communication is based on a debatable classification from the start.

Second, no one has yet been able to prove that "literature" should be interpreted by a different set of rules than other writings. There is no convincing answer to the question "Why should this written work be interpreted differently from other written works?" Surely the burden of proof lies with those who would argue that a particular written work (arbitrarily called "literature") should be interpreted differently from the way all other works (nonliterature) should be interpreted. Yet such a proof has not been demonstrated.

To deny that the author determines the text's meaning also raises an ethical question. Such an approach appears to rob the author of his or her creation. To treat a text in complete isolation from its author's intended purpose is like stealing a patent from its inventor or a child from the parent who gave it birth. If we list a work under the name of its author, we are at least tacitly admitting that it "belongs" to its author. He or she "owns" this work. To take it and place upon it our own meaning is a kind of plagiarism. There is a sense in which we have stolen what belongs to someone else. A text is like a "will" the author leaves for his or her heirs. It is mischievous to interpret such a will and ignore the intention of its author. For a will's executor to ignore what the author intended by his or her will is criminal and violates everyone's sense of fairness. For an interpreter to do the same with an author's literary work likewise seems unethical and disrespectful of the willed legacy of the author.

Objections to the Author as the Determiner of Meaning

Several objections have been raised against the view that the meaning of a text is determined by the author, and that in seeking the meaning of a text we are in essence trying to understand what an author like Paul consciously willed to communicate by his text. One of the most famous of these objections is called the "intentional fallacy." This objection, made famous by William K. Wimsatt Jr. and Monroe Beardsley, argues that it is impossible to climb into the mind of an author, such as Paul, and experience everything that was going through his mind as he wrote. A reader can never relive the experiences of the author. The innermost emotions, feelings, and motives Paul had as he wrote are simply not accessible to the reader, unless the author chose to reveal them in his text. As a result of such considerations, it is argued that the meaning Paul willed is inaccessible.

But when reading a Pauline text, the primary goal is not to experience or reduplicate Paul's mental and emotional experiences when he wrote. Rather the goal is to understand what Paul "meant," what he consciously sought to communicate to his readers by what he wrote. This objection confuses two different aspects of communication. The first involves the mental and emotional acts experienced by Paul; the second involves what Paul wanted to communicate. A careful distinction must be made between what Paul wished to convey in his text and the mental, emotional, and psychological experiences he went through while writing. What Paul sought to convey by his text is in the public realm, for he purposely made this available to the reader in the text itself. On the other hand, the inner mental and emotional experiences of Paul, or his "mental acts," are private and not accessible to the reader, unless Paul explicitly revealed them in his text. The goal of interpretation is not to relive Paul's emotional and mental state, but to understand what he meant by the written text he gave us. The intentional fallacy appears to confuse the meaning of a text with the experiences of the writer as he wrote. A text means what an author such as Paul wished to convey by his words. We have access to this because we have access to Paul's words. We do not have access to his mental acts.

The intentional fallacy has also argued that an author at times may intend to convey a particular meaning but be incapable of adequately expressing this. The author may be linguistically incompetent. All of us at some time or other have realized that we may not have expressed adequately what we wished to communicate. Even very capable communicators can at times fail to express correctly what they meant. It is therefore quite possible that an author could fail to express in an understandable way what he or she sought to communicate. Authors could even mislead the reader by a poor or wrong choice of words. This objection, however, tends to be more hypothetical than real. Most writers, such as Paul, possess sufficient literary competence to express their thoughts adequately. In fact, those who write articles outlining this problem and drawing it to their readers' attention usually think that they are sufficiently competent to express their thoughts quite adequately. If they did not, why would they write? Why then deny this competence to other writers?

For the Christian, an additional factor comes into play at this point. The belief that the Bible is inspired introduces a component of divine enabling into the situation. If in the writing of Scripture the authors were "moved by the Holy Spirit" (2 Pet. 1:21), then it would appear that the authors of the Bible were given a divine competence in writing. This competence enabled them to express adequately the revelatory matters they wanted to communicate in their writing.

Another objection to the view that the reader should seek the authorial meaning of the text involves the psychological differences between the author and the reader. Since the psychological makeup of each individual is unique, it is argued that a reader cannot understand the thoughts, emotions, and feelings the author possessed when he or she wrote. The reader is simply too different psychologically. As a result, a reader can never understand what an author truly meant by his or her text.

A related objection is the view that a modern reader is not able to understand the meaning of an ancient author such as Paul. The radical difference between the present situation of the reader and that of the author does not permit this. How can the modern-day reader, familiar with computers and megabytes, jet airplanes and international travel, television, heart transplants, lunar landings, and nuclear power understand an ancient author writing thousands of years ago in a time of sandals, togas, and animal sacrifices? According to this view, the culture of the author and the culture of the reader are so radically different that it is impossible for a present-day reader to understand what an ancient

writer meant. The author and reader live too many centuries, even millennia, apart.

These objections are well taken, and should not be minimized. The
differences between the time and thought-world of an ancient author
and the modern reader are very real. Far too often we tend to mod-
ernize ancient writers and assume that they thought exactly like twentieth-century Americans. Consequently we misunderstand them. On
the other hand, we can also overemphasize these differences. After all,
we are not trying to understand the thoughts of worms or toads! The
common humanity we share with the authors of the past and the fact
that we both have been created in the image of God facilitate bridging
this gap of time. The basic needs for food, clothing, warmth, security,
love, and forgiveness the ancients had are still the basic needs we have
today. Thus, while difficult, understanding an ancient author is not
impossible. In a similar fashion the common possession of the image of
God assists in overcoming the psychological differences between the
author and reader as well.

One final objection that can be raised with regard to the interpretation of the Bible involves those texts in which an author appeals to a
faith experience. How can an atheist or unbeliever understand the meaning of the psalmist when he states, "Blessed is he whose transgressions
are forgiven, whose sins are covered. Blessed is the man whose sin the
LORD does not count against him and in whose spirit is no deceit. When
I kept silent, my bones wasted away through my groaning all day long.
For day and night your hand was heavy upon me" (Ps. 32:1–4a).
Whereas a believer may be able to understand the experience of faith
that the author is talking about, how can an atheist? We must, however,
distinguish here between understanding what the author means by these
words and understanding the subject matter he is discussing. An atheist
can understand that the psalmist is talking about the joy of being forgiven
by the LORD and the personal agony that preceded this. On the other
hand, an atheist cannot understand the experience, the subject matter, of
which the psalmist is speaking. He or she may in fact seek to explain that
subject matter via Freudian psychology because of not being able to accept
the divine element involved in it. Yet an atheist can understand what the
psalmist means by his discussion of this issue. The psalmist is speaking
of the agony of guilt and the joy of forgiveness. An atheist, however,
can never understand the truth of the subject matter, the experience,
of which the psalmist speaks. (For further discussion, see pp. 65–71.)

The Role of the Author

Texts do not simply appear in history. They do not evolve from trees or from papyrus plants or from animal skins. An ancient text did not come into existence because some animal lost its skin or some papyrus plant shed its bark and written symbols miraculously appeared on them. Someone, some time, somewhere wanted to write these texts. Someone, some time, somewhere willed to say something and have others read it. If this were not true, these texts would never have appeared. A thinking person consciously willed to write a text for the purpose of conveying something meaningful to the reader. Since this took place in past time, what the author willed to convey by the linguistic symbols used (whether the symbols were Hebrew, Aramaic, Greek, or Latin is immaterial) possesses a meaning that can never change. What a biblical author willed by his text is anchored in history. It was composed in the past, and being part of the past, what the author willed to communicate back then can never change. What a text meant when it was written, it will always mean. It can no more change than any other event of the past can change, because its meaning is forever anchored in past history.

Yet what an author such as Paul consciously willed to say in the past also has implications of which he was not necessarily aware. Those implications are also part of the meaning of the text. When, for instance, Paul wrote in Ephesians 5:18, "Do not get drunk on wine," he was consciously thinking that the Ephesian Christians should not become intoxicated with the mixture of water and wine (usually two to three parts water to one part wine) that they called "wine." This saying, however, has implications that go beyond what Paul was consciously thinking. Paul gave a principle or pattern of meaning that has implications about not becoming drunk with beer, whiskey, rum, vodka, or champagne. If asked, Paul would state that although he was not consciously thinking of these other alcoholic beverages, he meant for Christians not to become drunk by using them as well. Certainly no one in Ephesus would have thought, "Paul in his letter forbids our becoming drunk with wine, but I guess it would not be wrong to become drunk with beer." Paul's text has implications that go beyond his own particular conscious meaning at the time. These implications do not conflict with his original meaning. On the contrary, they are included in that pattern of meaning he wished to communicate. It is true that they go beyond his conscious thinking when he wrote, but they are included in the principle Paul wished to communicate in this verse. Thus, what an author of Scripture stated in the past frequently has implications with respect to things of which he was not aware or did not even exist at the time the text was written!

The purpose of biblical interpretation involves not just understanding the specific conscious meaning of the author but also the principle or pattern of meaning he sought to communicate. If Paul did in fact prohibit becoming drunk with whiskey and modern-day alcoholic beverages, does he also forbid in Ephesians 5:18 the unnecessary use and abuse of narcotics? That other statements of Scripture forbid the abuse of the human body in such a manner is clear. But does this specific passage forbid its use? If we understand Paul's command as a principle, then it would appear that this passage does indeed prohibit the use of narcotics. If the principle or pattern of meaning willed by Paul in this saying is something like "Do not take into your body substances like wine that cause you to lose control of your senses and natural inhibitions," then the use of narcotics is likewise prohibited by this verse. If we were able to ask Paul about this latter instance, would he not reply, "I was not consciously thinking of narcotics when I wrote, but that's exactly the kind of thing I meant"? The fact is that every text has implications or unconscious meanings its author was not aware of but which fit the meaning willed in the text. More often than not, the main concern of interpretation is to understand what the legitimate implications of an author's meaning are.

We might pause for a moment to consider whether Jesus was thinking along these lines when he said, "You have heard that it was said to the people long ago, 'Do not murder . . . ' but I tell you . . . " or "You

Paul—Ephesians 5:18

have heard that it was said, 'Do not commit adultery.' But I tell you
. . . " (Matt. 5:21–48). It appears that Jesus here describes what is
involved in the higher righteousness referred to in Matthew 5:20 by
bringing out the implications of Moses' commandments. Whether
Moses was consciously thinking of these implications when he wrote
these commandments is immaterial. They are legitimate implications
of the principles he wished to convey in them. At this point someone
might raise the following objection: "But isn't God the author of Scripture?" This sounds devout enough, but Scripture does not claim God
as its immediate author. Paul's letters do not begin, "God, the Father,
Son, and Holy Spirit, to the church at Rome." No book of the Bible
claims God as its immediate author! Christians, of course, believe that
behind the books of the Bible stands the living God, who has inspired
his servants in the writing of these works. But the Scriptures were
written by men, not God. As a result, to understand the meaning of
the biblical texts we must understand what their human authors consciously willed to convey by their texts. The divine meaning of the
biblical texts is the conscious willed meaning of God's inspired
prophets and apostles. To understand the divine meaning of Scripture, then, is to understand the conscious meaning of God's inspired
servants who wrote them. It is in, not behind or beyond, the meaning the author wished to share that we find the meaning God wished
to share in the Scriptures!

The term "conscious" has been used on numerous occasions with respect to the willed meaning of the author. Although this may seem awkward, it has been used intentionally. The reason for this is to avoid two errors. One involves those interpreters who argue that "myths" are present throughout the Bible. According to this view the miracle stories found in Scripture are to be understood not as historical accounts, but as fictional stories or myths. The meanings of these myths, they argue, are "subconscious" truths and Christian values that were at play in the subconscious thinking of the early church and the Christian writers. Thus the meanings of these "myths" are not found in what the authors of Scripture consciously sought to express in the pattern of meaning they wrote. The "meaning" of these myths were, on the contrary, totally unknown to them and are independent of any conscious pattern of meaning they wished to convey. The meaning lies in their subconsciousness, which gave rise to these myths. They were, however, completely unaware of this. Attributing the meaning of a text to the "conscious" willed meaning of the author avoids this error.

The term "subconsciousness" must not be confused with what is referred to as the "unconscious" meaning of the text. "Unconscious" meanings, or implications, are indeed unknown to the author, but they fall within his conscious, willed pattern of meaning. The "subconscious" meaning sought in this mythical approach, however, has nothing to do with what the author consciously wished to convey. In fact, it is usually quite opposed to the author's willed meaning, because the author believed in the facticity of the events he was reporting and wished to share the meaning of those events with his readers. (This will be discussed at greater length in chapter 2 under Implications.)

On the opposite extreme are those who argue that the Bible must be interpreted literally at all times. This, too, is an error, for it loses sight of the fact that the biblical writers used various literary forms in their works such as proverbs, poetry, hyperbole, and parables. They never intended that their readers should interpret such passages literally. They intended for them to be interpreted according to the literary rules associated with such forms. Thus, the conscious willed meaning of Jesus when he said, "If anyone comes to me and does not hate his father and mother, his wife and children, his brothers and sisters—yes, even his own life—he cannot be my disciple" (Luke 14:26), is not that his disciples must literally hate their parents. It means rather that to be disciples of Jesus we must place him before everything and everyone. The meaning of Luke 14:26 is therefore what Jesus and Luke consciously sought to communicate by these words and not the literal meaning of the words. Similarly, the parable of the rich man and Lazarus (Luke 16:19–31) is to be interpreted as a parable, and thus according to the rules governing the interpretation of parables. It is not to be interpreted as a historical account. (Luke reveals this by the introduction "A certain man . . . " which is used in the Gospel to introduce parables [cf. Luke 10:30; 14:16; 15:11; 16:1; 19:12]. This is clearer in the Greek text than in most translations, but it is fairly obvious in the NASB.)

The Role of the Text

A text consists of a collection of verbal symbols. These symbols can be various kinds of letters, punctuation marks, accents (Greek), or vowel pointing (Hebrew). A biblical author could have used any symbols he wanted to write his text. In fact, he could have invented a language that only he, and those whom he chose, knew. Special codes are created for this purpose. A secret code is a text that authors want to keep hidden from others; they will reveal the meaning only to those who know the "code." In times of war such codes are especially important. When others "break" that code, as U.S. naval intelligence did in World War II at the Battle of Midway, this may have disastrous consequences for those assuming that only their side understands the code.

However, if an author wishes to convey meaning to as many people as possible, as the biblical authors did, then he or she will choose a code, a collection of verbal symbols, which the readers will understand. This code will involve consonants, vowels, punctuation, words, idioms, and grammar that the author and readers share in common. In writing, an author therefore creates a text that possesses "shareability." Shareability is the common understanding of a text's words and grammar possessed by both author and reader. Apart from this a reader cannot understand what an author wills to say. As a result an author purposely submits himself or herself to the conventions and understanding of language possessed by the readers. Thus, if we understand how the author's intended audience would have understood the text, we, as readers today, can also understand the meaning of that same text. Because we can learn how a contemporary of Paul would have understood the Greek words (vocabulary), grammatical construction (syntax), and context of the text, we can also understand Paul's meaning, for the apostle purposely submitted himself to the norms of the language of his readers.

Because of the need for shareability, an author will abide by the "norms of language" and use words and grammar in a way familiar to his audience. If he uses a word in an unfamiliar way, a good author will explain this in some way to his reader. (Cf. how the author of Hebrews explains what he means in 5:14a by "mature" in 5:14b; how John explains what Jesus meant in 2:19–20 by "temple" in 2:21; and what he meant by 7:37–38 in 7:39.) Within the norms of language, however, words possess a range of possible meanings. We can find this range of meanings in a dictionary or lexicon. An author is aware, when he uses his words, that they must possess one of these meanings. But when he uses these words, the context he gives to them narrows down the possible meanings to just one—the specific meaning found in the statement itself.

For example, the word "love" can mean a number of things. It can mean such things as profoundly tender, passionate affection; warm personal attachment; sexual intercourse; strong predilection or liking; a score of zero in tennis; a salutation in a letter. In the sentence "He lost six-love," however, it can only mean a zero score in tennis. The sentence "Let us love one another," on the other hand, is quite ambiguous. It can mean one thing when found in the context of Jesus' teachings and quite another thing in the context of a pornographic magazine. Through the specific context an author provides his verbal symbols—the sentence in which these symbols occur, the paragraph in which they are found, the chapter in which he places them—he reveals the specific meaning of his words. Linguists sometimes use the French word *langua* to describe the range of possibilities that a word possesses in the norms of language and the French word *parole* to describe the specific meaning of the word as it is used within the sentence, that is, the norms of the utterance.

Because of the shareability of the verbal symbols the biblical author uses, a text can communicate his meaning. A text, however, can communicate a great deal more. A text can open up to the reader vast areas of information. By reading a text a reader may learn all sorts of historical, psychological, sociological, cultural, and geographical information. A text can be a storehouse of information, "subject matter," and a reader can investigate a text to acquire such information. We can read the Gospel of Mark, for instance, to learn about the history of Jesus, about the shape and form of the Jesus traditions before they were written down, about the Markan literary style. We can study the Book of Joshua to learn about the geography of Palestine or second-millennium military strategy. We can study the Psalms to learn about ancient Hebraic poetry or Israelite worship. All this is both possible and frequently worthwhile, but when this is done, we should always be aware of the fact that this is not the study of the text's meaning. The meaning of those texts is what the authors of Mark, Joshua, and the Psalms willed to teach their readers by recounting this history, these traditions, this geography, this poetic form.

As a result, when investigating an account such as Jesus calming the storm (Mark 4:35–41), we must be careful to focus our attention on the meaning of the account rather than on its various subject matters. The purpose of this account is not to help the reader acquire information concerning the topography of the Sea of Galilee (a lake surrounded by a ring of high hills) and how this makes it prone to sudden, violent storms (4:37). Nor is it primarily about the lack of faith on the part of the disciples (4:40) or the shape and size of boats on the Sea of Galilee in the first century (4:37). On the contrary, Mark has revealed in the opening verse of his Gospel that this work is about "Jesus Christ, the Son of God." This account, therefore, should be interpreted in light of this. The meaning that Mark sought to convey is also clear from the account itself. The account reaches its culmination in the concluding statement, "Who is this? Even the wind and the waves obey him!" (4:41). The meaning of this account, what Mark sought to convey, is therefore that Jesus of Nazareth is the Christ, the Son of God. He is the Lord, and even nature itself is subject to his voice!

Perhaps the greatest need in reading the Bible is to distinguish the vast amount of information that we can learn from the biblical texts from the meaning the authors give to that information. This will be dealt with at greater length in succeeding chapters. (See especially pp. 46–48.)

The Role of the Reader

Using the verbal symbols of the author, that is, the text, the reader seeks to understand what the author meant by these symbols. Knowing that the author intentionally used shareable symbols, the reader begins with the knowledge that the individual building blocks of the text, the words, fit within the norms of the language of the original readers. (This means that in reading the works of Shakespeare we must use a sixteenth- rather than a twentieth-century English dictionary!) Seeing how the words are used in phrases and sentences, and how the sentences are used within paragraphs, and how paragraphs are used in chapters, and how chapters are used in the work, the reader seeks to understand the author's intent in writing this work. This process is called the "hermeneutical circle." This expression refers to the fact that the whole text helps the reader understand each individual word or part of the text; at the same time the individual words and parts help us understand the meaning of the text as a whole. This sounds more confusing than it really is, for all this goes on simultaneously in the mind of the interpreter. The mind is able to switch back and forth from the part to the whole without great difficulty. It functions like a word processor in which the computer switches back and forth at great speed when copying from disc to disc. Similarly, the mind switches back and forth from the meaning of the individual words and the general understanding of the whole text until it comes to a successful resolution of the text's meaning.

Because the reader is interested in what a biblical author meant by his text, he or she is interested in his other writings as well, for these are especially helpful in providing clues to the meaning of the words and phrases in his text. Other works written by people of similar conviction and language are also helpful, especially if they were written at the same time. The writings of people who had different convictions but lived at the same time may also be helpful, but less so, in revealing the norms of language under which the author worked. As a result, to understand what Paul means in a particular verse in Romans the reader should look at the way he thinks and writes in the verses surrounding that text, in the neighboring chapters, in the rest of that book, then in Galatians (which is the Pauline writing most like Romans), then in 1 and 2 Corinthians, and then in the other Pauline writings. After hav-

Resources

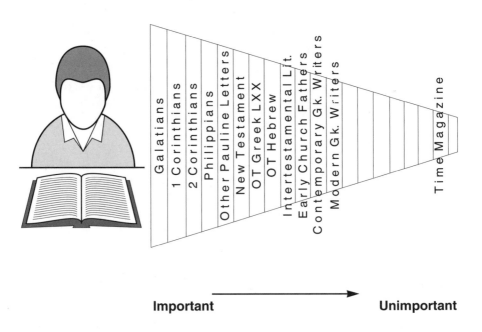

Important   Unimportant

ing worked through the Pauline materials, the reader can also else-where. Probably the order of importance after the Pauline materials would be: the rest of the New Testament; the Old Testament; the intertestamental literature; the rabbinic literature; the early church fathers; contemporary Greek literature. (This order would be determined by which of the others best reflects the way Paul thought.) In a similar way a verse in the Gospel of Luke is best interpreted by the verses surrounding it, the paragraphs and chapters surrounding that verse, the rest of the Gospel of Luke, and then the Book of Acts. Acts would reveal better how Luke thought than Matthew, Mark, or John, but other Gospels would be better than Isaiah, which in turn would be better than Josephus, a Jewish historian of the first century.

It is also important for the reader to understand the particular literary form being used by the author, for different forms of literature are governed by different rules. If the author has expressed his willed meaning in the form of a proverb, we must then interpret that proverb by the rules governing this literary form. If he has used a parable, we must interpret the parable in light of the rules associated with parables. The careful argumentation of Paul in Romans must be interpreted differently from the poetic form in which the psalmist has expressed his meaning. What is common in the interpretation of every literary form, however, is that we are in each instance seeking to understand the meaning the author willed. Furthermore, we can assume that, since he sought to share that meaning with his readers, he was abiding by the common rules associated with the particular literary form he was using.

Once the reader knows the meaning of the author, he or she will need to seek out those implications of that meaning that are especially relevant. If the pattern of meaning Paul willed when he wrote Ephesians 5:18 is "Do not take into your body substances like alcohol that cause you to lose control of your senses and natural inhibitions," what implications arising out of this paradigm of meaning are most relevant for the reader? Because Paul's text has far-reaching implications that he was not aware of, the value of a text, its "significance," is multiple and varied. Although the meaning of a text never changes because it is locked in past history, its significance is always changing. This is why some people claim that the Scriptures have different "meanings." Yet a text does not have different "meanings," for an author like Paul willed a single specific pattern of meaning when he wrote. (The instances in which an author willed a "double meaning" pun are quite rare.) A text, however, has different "significances" for different readers. For example, the words of Jesus, "and you will be my witnesses in Jerusalem, and in all Judea and Samaria, and to the ends of the earth" (Acts 1:8), have a single meaning. Jesus wanted to see the message of the gospel spread throughout the entire world. Yet the value of various implications, the significance of Jesus' words, will no doubt vary a great deal for each reader. For me it involves teaching in a theological seminary; for my daughter and son-in-law it involves going overseas to a foreign land to work among an unreached people; for my sons and their wives it involves working in their local churches. For others it may involve working in a rural church or in the inner city or witnessing about Christ at work. For a non-Christian it no doubt would involve a rejection of the meaning. There is one meaning to a text, that meaning consciously willed by the author, but the particular way that meaning affects the readers, its significance, will be quite different.

Questions

1. Is there such a thing as "the meaning" of a text? If so, where is this meaning to be found? Who or what determines it?

2. How can we determine what constitutes a good translation of the Bible? Does this have any bearing on what is discussed in this chapter?

3. Why do people learn Greek and Hebrew (and Aramaic) in order to study the Bible? What does this say about where a text's meaning is to be found?

4. In the desire to communicate their message, how do writers restrict themselves? How does this restriction aid us in interpreting the Bible?

2

Defining the Rules:
A Vocabulary
for Interpretation

One of the major problems encountered in interpreting
the Bible is imprecise terminology. If the terms used in
the process of interpretation are used imprecisely, confusion will result.
This is even more so if the same term is used in different or contradictory
ways. One of the values of a precise vocabulary is that it helps us obtain
a clearer picture of what is involved in the process of interpretation.
Such a vocabulary also enables us to understand better what others are
saying when they use less accurate terminology. This is because we can
retranslate their terminology into our clearer terminological framework.

This works well in other areas also. For example, in the study of theology it is very helpful to master a theological system such as Calvinism,
even if one is not a Calvinist. If we know this theological system well,
we can then compare other theological views to this known system. As
a result, the new theological views will become clear, because they are
being compared to a known theological system. Similarly, it is easier to
understand how other governments function if we possess a clear understanding of how our own government functions. This will permit us to
make comparisons such as "Their X functions like our House of Rep-
resentatives, but they do not have a Senate." In this chapter a precise
hermeneutical vocabulary will be presented so we will better understand what is involved in the process of interpretation.

Meaning

The meaning of a text is that pattern of meaning the author willed to convey by the words (shareable symbols) he used.

It should be noted that all three components of communication are present in this definition. The *author* is represented in that he or she wills the meaning of the text. The *text* is represented by the symbols the author uses to express the meaning. The *reader* is represented by the shareable nature of those symbols, for the author wrote with the reader in mind and purposely submitted himself or herself to the norms of the language with which the reader was familiar.

The meaning of a text depends on the specific conscious will of the author. The biblical author is the determiner of the text's meaning. Since this pattern of meaning was willed in the past (when the text was written), the meaning of a text can never change, for it is locked in history. It can no more change than any other historical event of the past can change. Even the author cannot change the meaning of the text, because he cannot change the past. An author may "recant" of the meaning, but this does not alter the fact that the text still means what the author willed it to mean when the text was written. If an author wishes to change this meaning, he will produce a revision or new edition to express this new willed meaning. He cannot, however, make the old text mean something different now. The very fact that such recantations produce new revisions or editions is tacit testimony to the fact that the willed meaning of the old text cannot change.

Having said this, it should also be noted that what the biblical author meant has implications of which he was not aware. Every law has implications of which the original lawmakers were not aware. The task of the courts is to determine what the implications of these laws are. The original framers of the Constitution were not consciously aware of all the legitimate implications of the various articles that they included in this great work. These implications are nevertheless part of the meaning of this great text, and the role of the Supreme Court is to discover the implications of the Constitution. In the same manner the authors of Scripture, who were led by the Spirit, willed implications that go far beyond the specific meaning they consciously sought to convey when they wrote.

Implications

Implications are those meanings in a text of which the author was unaware but nevertheless legitimately fall within the pattern of meaning he willed.

The specific meaning that an author like Paul willed is only the tip of the iceberg of his meaning. Far more of the pattern of meaning willed by the apostle lies below the surface than above. Most visible, of course, is the specific meaning Paul consciously sought to convey. Yet this specific meaning involves a pattern of meaning that contains numerous implications, and Paul was not aware of the majority of them. Of course, the specific meaning of Paul lies within his pattern of meaning, but that specific meaning is only part of all the submeanings contained in that pattern. Paul, for instance, in the pattern of meaning willed in Ephesians 5:18, prohibited drunkenness that results from drinking any alcoholic beverage, not just wine. The command not to be drunk with wine

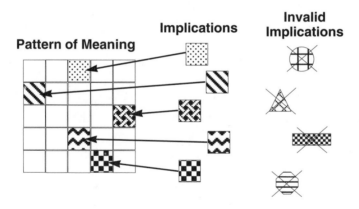

(Note: The Pattern of Meaning is represented by a square and the implications are therefore subsquares that fit the "squareness" of the Pattern of Meaning.)

is part of that pattern of meaning. But that pattern also involves all later alcoholic beverages, and narcotics as well. Although Paul was thinking primarily of "drinking" wine, he also meant by implication becoming drunk by taking alcoholic beverages or drugs intravenously, even though he had no idea of how such substances could enter the body in this manner.

Other terms that can be used to describe these implications are sub-meanings or subtypes. The term "unconscious meaning" is still another synonym although, if we want to be precise, it is somewhat less inclusive than the term "implication." The reason for this is that an author may when writing be conscious of various implications of his specific meaning even though he does not state them. Thus, Paul was no doubt aware that Ephesians 5:18 also forbids being drunk from beer, because this was an existing alcoholic beverage. The term "implication" would include this submeaning but not the term "unconscious meaning." In practice, however, these terms are for the most part interchangeable.

The goal of biblical interpretation is to understand not just the specific meaning of the authors of Scripture but also, by understanding their willed pattern of meaning, to understand the various implications. These implications are not "determined" by the interpreter, however. On the contrary, they are determined by the author. By his willed pattern of meaning the biblical author has delineated what the implications of his meaning are. The interpreter of Scripture ascertains or discovers these implications, but it is the author alone who has determined them. The interpreter seeks to discover the various implications of the author's willed type much like a miner digs into a mountain to discover gold. Even as a miner does not make the gold in the mountain, so the interpreter does not make the implications of a text's meaning. Both seek to discover what is already there. The miner seeks to discover the gold that God created and that lies in the mountain. Similarly, the interpreter seeks to discover the implications that the biblical author created and that lie in his willed pattern of meaning. For both, what they seek lies in a past event of creation. Just as God has created the gold in the past, so the author has created the implications of his meaning in the past.

The legitimate implications of a statement such as "Oak trees are wonderful" are determined by the author who spoke/wrote it and the context he or she provided. Thus, if it was spoken by a child climbing a tree, a contractor building a house, an artist painting a landscape, a civil engineer in charge of flood control, or a biologist teaching photosynthesis, the implications will be quite different. For a child an implication such as "Oak trees are wonderful for climbing because of their many branches" would be legitimate, whereas the strength and beauty of oak trees for housing construction, the beautiful proportions of a certain oak tree, the value of oak trees for preventing erosion and for breaking the momentum of a flooded river, or the ability of an oak tree to convert nutrients through photosynthesis would not be. On the other hand, these other implications may be legitimate for a contractor, an artist, an engineer, or a biologist. Which of these possible implications flow justifiably from the meaning "Oak trees are wonderful" will be determined not by the reader, however, but by the speaker whose willed meaning is accessible from the context he or she provides.

An example of how this works is found in Galatians 5:2. There Paul states, "Mark my words! I, Paul, tell you that if you let yourselves be circumcised, Christ will be of no value to you at all." The specific meaning that Paul has in mind is clear. He wants the Galatian Christians to know that, if they as Gentiles submit to being circumcised under pressure from the Judaizers, they will have renounced their faith. They will have rejected trusting alone on God's grace in Christ and sought instead to establish a different relationship with God, one that depends ultimately on their own actions or works, on their having submitted to circumcision. Paul wants his readers to know that they cannot mix a faith that rests on God's grace alone and a righteousness of works. For the Gentiles in Galatia to accept circumcision is therefore the equivalent of renouncing Christ!

Yet such a specific teaching is of little value today, unless Paul willed a pattern of meaning by this teaching that has implications of which he was not aware. Circumcision is not an issue within the Christian church today. Yet throughout the history of the church, the implications of this verse have proven most useful. Luther saw a very relevant implication for his day. He saw buying indulgences or doing penance as a sixteenth-century attempt to establish a relationship with God that depended on one's own actions. It was to renounce the biblical relationship that rests on God's grace and is mediated by faith alone. Certainly Paul was not thinking of the sixteenth-century abuse of indulgences or works of penance when he wrote Galatians, but Luther was correct in seeing that this is an implication contained in Paul's meaning.

I remember very clearly a situation when the implications of this text were extremely relevant for me. Confronted by some religious zealots who warned me that to be saved I needed to worship on a particular day of the week, I responded, "My only hope of salvation is that when I stand before God, he will remember that Jesus died for me and that because of his atoning death, he will forgive me. Are you saying that if I do not worship on the day you worship, God will not accept me?" Their reply was, "If you do not worship on our day due to ignorance,

God may forgive you." To this I quickly replied, "But I am not doing this out of ignorance. I worship on the first day of the week because this is what the early church did." "Then," they responded, "you are damned!" The implications of this Pauline text are very relevant. We cannot mix grace/faith with works of law. It is by faith alone, not faith plus circumcision, not faith plus indulgences, not faith plus penance, not faith plus sabbath worship, that we are saved.

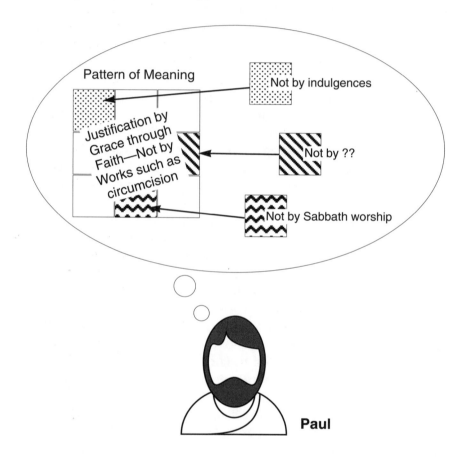

In a similar way the commands not to kill and not to commit adultery in Exodus 20:13–14 have implications that go beyond the conscious meaning of the biblical author. Jesus understood this when he said that anger violated the meaning of the command not to kill and that to look on a woman lustfully violated the meaning of the command not to commit adultery. Thus, Jesus in Matthew 5:21–48 was not contradicting the meaning of Moses' words in Exodus. Rather he was bringing out various implications that lie in the willed pattern of Moses' meaning. Similarly, the commandment "an eye for and eye and a tooth for a tooth" found in Exodus 21:23–25 has such unconscious meanings as not cutting off the hand of a person for stealing a loaf of bread and not executing a person for killing a deer in the king's forest preserve. This is because the intended pattern of meaning was that punishment should befit the crime. Cutting off a hand for stealing a loaf of bread or executing a person for killing a deer on the king's preserve are much too excessive and go far, far beyond a penalty befitting the crime.

It is evident that the meaning of a text goes beyond the specific conscious meaning of its author. The meaning, which an author wills, includes all the implications or unconscious meanings contained in the pattern (or type) he is teaching. It includes both the conscious meaning that the author willed by his shareable symbols and all the implications that fit within this pattern or type. This is why the implications of the biblical writers can go far beyond their conscious thinking at the time. These implications, however, are controlled and bounded by the writer's willed meaning. If we visualize Paul's pattern of meaning in Galatians 5:2 as a large square, then only those possible submeanings that are also square in nature are legitimate. Circular submeanings are not legitimate; nor are triangular submeanings. Similarly, if the pattern of meaning willed in Ephesians 5:18 is visualized as rectangular in nature, then only those possible submeanings that are rectangular in nature are valid implications. It is necessary, therefore, to have a clear and carefully defined understanding of the willed pattern of the author in order to delimit the true implications of the text. Thus, whereas alcoholic and narcotic substances fit within the meaning of Ephesians 5:18 in that they cause people to become "intoxicated," to lose control of their behavior, overeating or overworking do not. There may be other texts of Scripture that speak about overeating or overworking, but the pattern of meaning willed by Paul in Ephesians 5:18 does not.

Significance

Significance refers to how a reader responds to the meaning of a text.

For Christians there is a close relationship between the significance and the implications of a biblical text. The reason for this is that Christians attribute positive significance to the implications of such texts. But a non-Christian might agree that "X" and "Y" are legitimate implications of a biblical text and simply say, "I don't believe this!" or "So what! I don't care!" Significance involves a person's attitude toward the meaning of a text. It is a critique of the author's willed meaning. (Another way of saying this is that significance is the effect that the text's meaning has on the reader.) It may be positive, but it may also be negative. Because Christians believe that the Bible is the Word of God, a legitimate implication of the meaning of a biblical text usually has positive significance.

Frequently people make a distinction between what a text meant and what a text means. (Sometimes the terms "meaning" and "meaningfulness" are used.) The former refers to what the biblical author meant when he wrote the text, his willed pattern of meaning. The latter, on the other hand, refers to the application of the text for the present-day reader. Such terminology, although popular, can be confusing, because the verb "mean" is used in two quite different ways. For the sake of greater clarity, it is wiser to refer to the "meaning" of the text and the "significance" of the text. Meaning belongs to the author; significance belongs to the reader. Thus, the expression "what a text meant" will correspond to what is defined as "meaning" in this chapter. The expression "what a text means (to me) . . . " will not be used, but will be replaced by "The *significance* of this text (for me) is . . . "

It has been pointed out that there is only one meaning of a text, that of the author. Because it is located in the past, that meaning is unchangeable. Significance, however, is multifaceted. The significance of a text for one person may be quite different than its significance for another person. The significance of the Great Commission in Matthew 28:19–20 for one person may involve obeying one of its implications by becoming a pastor; for another it may involve obeying one of its implications by becoming a missionary; and for still another it may involve obeying one of its implications by witnessing to neighbors. All these are positive responses to legitimate implications of the willed pattern of meaning found in that commission, and they are all different. On the other hand, for some the meaning of this passage will be ignored or rejected. The meaning of the Great Commission, while singular, has numerous implications and invites many responses (i.e., significances).

The significance of a text's meaning must be distinguished from the implications of the text's meaning. Significance is something that read-

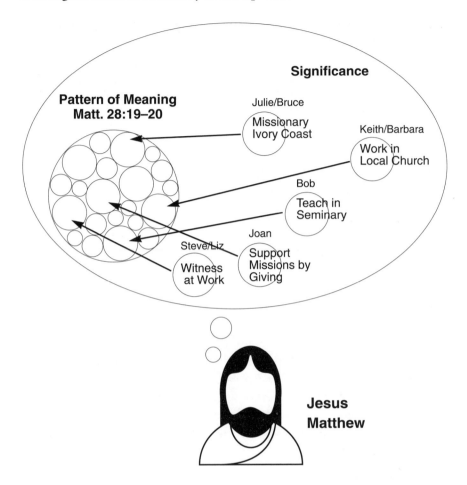

ers do as they respond to the meaning of the text. The interpreter is the master of significance, because he or she can say "Yes" or "No." Implications, however, lie outside the domain of the interpreter. They are determined by the author. They are only discovered or learned by the reader. Once discovered, however, the reader becomes master of the situation, for to these implications the reader can say "Yes" or "No." He or she can obey or reject them. We should not therefore confuse the implications of the author's willed meaning with the interpreter's response to those implications. Significance refers to the response of the interpreter and involves the will. It does not refer to the mind's perception of the various implications of the author's willed meaning. (The term "application" is sometimes used to describe "significance." For instance, when people speak of "the application of this text for me," they are referring to what we have here defined as "significance." Yet the term "application" can also be used to refer to "implication." We do this when we refer abstractly to the "various applications" of a text. We shall avoid this term because of its ambiguity and refer instead to "implication" and "significance.")

Subject Matter

Subject matter refers to the content or "stuff" talked about in a text.

The subject matter of a text involves the area of knowledge concerning which the text is speaking. Examples of subject matter are as follows:

Genesis 1–3—the creation of the world, ancient traditions about creation, the literary and oral sources used by the author, authorship, date, etc.

Ezra—the history of the Jews in the fifth century B.C., the political situation of the Middle East in that century, the geography or archaeology of Jerusalem, authorship, date, etc.

Psalms—Hebraic poetry, ancient Jewish liturgical formulas, Jewish worship, the classification of psalm forms, authorship, date, etc.

Proverbs—ancient Near Eastern wisdom literature, the literary genre of proverbs, authorship, date, etc.

Jeremiah—the history of Judah in the sixth century B.C., the life of Jeremiah, the literary genre of prophecy, how prophetic traditions were circulated, authorship, date, etc.

Gospels—the life of Jesus, the teaching of Jesus, the literary relationship of the Gospels, the classification of the Gospel pericopes, the history of the oral traditions, authorship, date, etc.

Galatians—Greek epistolary form, ancient genre of rhetoric, the geographical location of the Galatians, the chronology of Paul's life, the problem in Galatia, authorship, date, etc.

As can be seen from the above, a text can be investigated for numerous reasons. The ones listed are all legitimate and interesting areas of study, but none of these involves the meaning of the text. A clear distinction

Subject Matters

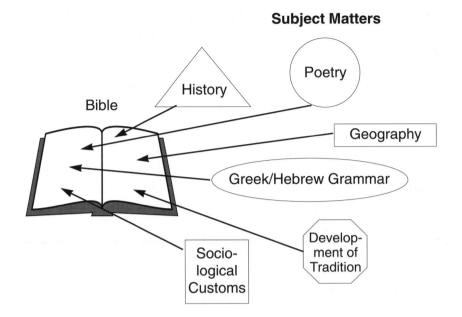

must be maintained between the subject matter found in the text and the meaning that the author gives to this subject matter.

An example may be helpful. In Mark 2:1–12 we find the account of the healing of the paralytic. This account contains a vast amount of subject matter that can be investigated. Some of this includes the historical questions of when in the life of Jesus this event occurred or what exactly took place (the quest for the historical Jesus); the architectural design and construction of first-century homes in Galilee; medical questions as to the kind and causes of paralysis in first-century Galilee; the relationship of illness and sin in Jewish theology; the form-critical classification of this account; the history of this account during the oral period of tradition; and so on. None of these, however, involves the meaning of this text.

The meaning of Mark 2:1–12 is what the Evangelist sought to teach by his use of this subject matter. What he sought to teach his readers by this passage is clear from Mark 1:1. The Gospel of Mark is about the "gospel about Jesus Christ, the Son of God." In the text itself this emphasis is seen in several places: in the question "'Why does this fellow talk like that? . . . Who can forgive sins but God alone?'" (2:7); in Jesus' statement that the Son of Man has authority to forgive sins (2:10); in the performance of a miracle to demonstrate this authority; and in the conclusion "'We have never seen anything like this!'" (2:12). Here lies the meaning of this text. Mark wants to show his readers by this text that Jesus is the Christ, the Son of God. There has never been anyone like him, for he has divine authority to forgive sins.

The meaning of this text involves the great christological truth that Jesus is the Son of God and possesses the divine authority to forgive sins. One legitimate implication (or unconscious meaning) is that Jesus is an all-sufficient Savior. Another is that Jesus has authority to forgive our sins. Still another is that Jesus is able, if he so wills, to heal us. On the other hand, the meaning of the text is not about building construction materials of the first century or whether we should classify this account as a miracle story or as a pronouncement story. The meaning willed by Mark concerns Jesus Christ, the Son of God, who has divine authority to heal and to forgive sins.

Frequently scholars make a distinction between the "text" and the "event." In this terminology, text is related to event as meaning is related to subject matter. When we are investigating the "text," we are seeking to ascertain what pattern or type of meaning the author willed to convey by his text. When we investigate the "event," we are investigating the historical subject matter referred to in the text. In studying the Gospels the investigation of the event involves learning what actually happened in the life of Jesus. When investigating the text, we are investigating what the Evangelist is seeking to teach by recounting this event in the life of Jesus. In other words, the "text" is the meaning the author attributes to the "event" (subject matter).

Understanding

Understanding refers to the correct mental grasp of the author's meaning.

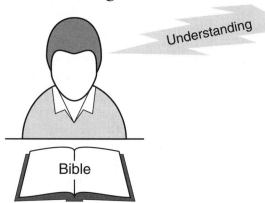

The understanding of a text involves the correct mental perception of a text's meaning. Another way of saying this is that understanding involves a correct grasp of the pattern of meaning willed by the author. Since there is a single meaning that the author willed, each individual who understands this meaning will have the same mental grasp of the author's pattern of meaning. Some understandings may be more complete than others because of a greater perception of the various implications involved, but, if an understanding is correct, it must have the same mental grasp of the author's meaning as any other understanding. Thus, although one person's understanding of meaning may be greater or more exhaustive than another's (because of a greater awareness of the various implications involved), every correct mental grasp of the author's meaning, or understanding, will be the same.

If we visualize the author's willed pattern of meaning as a circle, then every (correct) understanding grasps that the author willed a circle. Each person's understanding is the same—the author willed a circle. However, what is involved in that circle (all its implications) is not understood equally. Also, an individual's expression of that understanding (his or her "interpretation") will vary. One may express the meaning as a circle, another as a perfect roundness, another as a 360 degree curve, another as a two-dimensional sphere. Regardless of how this understanding may be expressed, every understanding involves a correct mental grasp of the meaning of the text.

Because understanding is defined as a "correct" mental grasp of meaning, there cannot be an "incorrect" understanding. This would be a contradiction of terms. To be precise we shall speak of an incorrect mental grasp of meaning as *mis*understanding. This will enable us to use the term "understanding" without qualification.

Interpretation

Interpretation refers to the verbal or written expression of a reader's understanding of the author's meaning.

Whereas there is a single meaning of a text and a single correct understanding of that meaning, there are an almost infinite number of ways of expressing this understanding. There are many ways of explaining the same perception of meaning. We can use different kinds of examples to express our understanding. In his ministry Jesus taught that the kingdom of God had come, but he used several different parables to teach this. We can also rephrase and use different vocabulary to express the same thought or understanding. The multiplicity of correct interpretations is demonstrated whenever we say something like, "Another way of saying this is . . . " or "Another example that will illustrate this is . . . " or "Perhaps a better way of stating this is . . . "

Some interpreters argue that there is no such thing as a perfect synonym. Yet an author can consciously will to use a synonym to mean the same thing as another term, because within the norms of language these synonyms can refer to the same thing. I have often used Roget's *Thesaurus* to find a synonym to express the same thing in order to avoid overusing the same word. Within the "norms of language" (see below) a word possesses a range of possible meanings. For the sake of analogy, let us conceive of the possible range of meanings as consisting of different circles. Two closely related words, such as "observe" and "see," have their own circle of meanings, but these two circles overlap. In these overlapping areas, "observe" and "see" can mean the same thing. Thus, an author can choose to select the same possible meaning for "observe" as for "see." He or she may mean the exact same thing by "I 'observed' the accident" as "I 'saw' the accident." Within this very chapter, I have done this; I have used "unconscious meaning," "submeaning," and "subtype" in order to avoid overusing the term "implication." In this book, these terms are synonyms.

Although understanding and interpretation are closely related, they are quite different. Understanding precedes interpretation. Understanding involves thinking and is "mental" whereas interpretation is "verbal." That they can be separated is witnessed to by those occasions when we "understand" something quite well but cannot find the words to express that understanding. For example, I understand what German-speaking people mean by the term *gemütlich*, but find it difficult to express this verbally.

Interpretation should not be confused with "translation." The latter is an attempt to express the conscious meaning of an author using the verbal symbols of another language. Because both interpretation and translation must be preceded by understanding and involve the verbal expression of that understanding, the boundary between them is vague and unclear. Translation seeks, however, to reproduce the meaning of the author as closely as possible in a different language; it seeks to restate the author's words in another language. Interpretation, on the other hand, need not involve two different languages and is free to use radically different images, terms, and metaphors to explain the meaning of an author.

Translation can be based on a "word-for-word" or a "thought-for-thought" philosophy. In the translation of the English Bible the Tyndale-Coverdale-Geneva-King James Version-American Standard Version-Revised Standard Version-New American Standard Bible-New Revised Standard Version followed a word-for-word philosophy in translating the biblical texts. (The New Revised Standard Version, however, in its attempt to be "nonsexist" tends to be more a thought-for-thought translation in the particular areas in which it sought to avoid sexist terminology.) Most of the popular modern translations, such as the New English Bible, the Revised English Bible, and the New International Version, follow the thought-for-thought model.

The weakness of the first approach is that no two languages and cultures have exact word equivalents. We need only attempt to translate Joseph's relationship to Mary in Matthew 1:18–20 to see this:

> Now the birth of Jesus Christ took place in this way. When his mother Mary had been betrothed to Joseph, before they came together she was found to be with child, of the Holy Spirit; and her husband Joseph, being a just man and unwilling to put her to shame, resolved to divorce her quietly. But as he considered this, behold, an angel of the Lord appeared to him in a dream, saying, "Joseph, son of David, do not fear to take Mary your wife, for that which is conceived in her is of the Holy Spirit." (RSV)

Were Joseph and Mary "betrothed" (1:18)? If so, why is he described as her "husband" (1:19)? Why is he considering "divorcing" his "wife" (1:19)? The problem is that we have no equivalent terms in our culture to describe the relationship of Joseph and Mary. In their culture they possessed a relationship that could only be broken by divorce (1:19). In this relationship any outside sexual relationship would have been considered adultery. However, no marriage ceremony had yet taken place (cf. Matt. 25:1–13), and there had been no sexual consummation (1:25). There are clearly no English terms that are exact equivalents to describe this situation. (We have a similar problem in trying to find an English equivalent for the German word *Gymnasium*. This describes a school, grades 4–13, which prepares students to enter the German university system. We have no equivalent English term. Furthermore, the fact that in German *Hochschule* ["high school"] refers more to what we would call college compounds the problem.)

The thought-for-thought model for translation also has its weaknesses. This is most evident when we seek to trace how an author uses the same terms in different places. The value of a concordance is compromised in such a translation even more than in a word-for-word translation. I have been frustrated on a number of occasions when I have referred to other passages in the NIV in which a biblical author uses the same word in the same way, but the NIV does not translate this word consistently. This is also a problem in a word-for-word translation but decidedly less so.

Mental Acts

Mental acts refer to the experiences the author went through when writing the text.

Although the pattern of meaning that an author willed to convey to readers is available through the text, his inner emotional and mental experiences are not. At times people confuse the meaning of a text with these mental acts. This is evident in the "intentional fallacy," which

Galatians 3:1ff.

states that it is impossible to reexperience what authors were going through when they wrote. When we are seeking the meaning of a text, however, we are not seeking to reexperience the mental acts of the author. We are interested rather in what the author wished to convey by the text that he has given us. Understanding what an author like Paul willed to convey by his words is quite understandable apart from knowing his mental acts while writing.

In an illuminating article entitled "Fern-seed and Elephants," C. S. Lewis warns against the attempt to reconstruct the mental acts of an author. In reviews of one of his earlier articles, various commentators speculated on what caused him to write this article and what was going through his mind as he wrote. This caused him to note how reviewers frequently had sought to reconstruct his writing experiences as well as the experiences of other authors whom he knew. He noted how reviewers, often with great confidence and certainty, spent a great deal of their reviews explaining what caused a particular author to write a work and what the circumstances were that gave rise to it. In analyzing such reconstructions of the mental acts of works by authors he knew well, as well as his own works, the impression of Lewis was that they were not simply wrong at times, or wrong half the time, but *always* wrong! He later qualified this somewhat by stating that this impression might be incorrect because he did not keep a written record, but he could not remember a single instance when reviewers were correct in regard to such speculations!

If Lewis is correct concerning the inability of critics, who were reared in the same country, culture, and educational system, to understand the mental acts of their contemporaries, this should give us pause. How then can we hope to understand what ancient authors were experiencing and the circumstances that led them to write? If contemporaries, who share the same culture and background, are not able to climb into the minds of present-day authors and ascertain their mental acts, how can we ever hope to do so with authors thousands of years ago whose culture, training, language, and worldview are radically different? What these authors consciously willed to convey to their readers we can know. Their willed meaning is available to us and can be understood, because we possess their texts. But their private experiences are not available. Unless an author chose to share such experiences with his readers, they are inaccessible, and Lewis rightly suggests that such investigation is highly speculative and of little value.

Norms of Language

The norms of language are the range of meanings allowed by the words (verbal symbols) of a text.

Within a language, a word can possess a range of possible meanings. This is seen most clearly in a dictionary in which the various meanings of words are listed. Although a word is limited to certain meanings, an author may choose any of these meanings listed in the dictionary. Authors cannot go outside these possibilities, however, if they wish to communicate with their readers. Since they want to be understood, they are willing to submit to these limitations. If they use a word in a way not permitted by the norms of language, they must reveal this to their readers or they will not be understood. The word "love," for example, has a limited range of possible meanings: "intense affectionate concern," "intense sexual desire," "strong fondness," "a zero score in tennis," "a complimentary close of a letter." The word "love" can mean any of these and many more, but it cannot mean "cheeseburger" or "dandruff." The norms of language, the standards of language, do not permit this.

Norms of Language
Dictionary

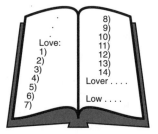

In a similar manner the norms of language permit a phrase such as "the love of Christ" to mean "the love of Christ for me" or "my love for Christ." The norms of language permit either. But it cannot mean "pumpkin pie and whipped cream." The term "faith" possesses a range of meanings in the New Testament. It can mean "a mere mental assent to a fact," "a wholehearted trust," or "a body of beliefs." The norms of language permit any of these possible meanings, but it does not permit "faith" to mean "computer programming."

Perhaps the classic example of this issue is found in Lewis Carroll's *Alice in Wonderland*. Alice and Humpty Dumpty have the following conversation:

> 'There's glory for you!' 'I don't know what you mean by "glory",' Alice said. Humpty Dumpty smiled contemptuously. 'Of course you don't— till I tell you. I meant "there's a nice knockdown argument for you"!' 'But "glory" doesn't mean "a nice knockdown argument",' Alice objected. 'When I use a word,' Humpty Dumpty said, in a rather scornful tone, 'it means just what I choose it to mean—neither more nor less.' 'The question is,' said Alice, 'whether you can *make* words mean so many different things.' 'The question is,' said Humpty Dumpty, 'which is to be master—that's all.'

There is a sense in which Humpty Dumpty is correct. He can make a word mean whatever he wants it to mean. But—and this is critical—if he wants to communicate his meaning to others, then he must submit himself to the norms of language. He can, of course, create a new word or a new meaning for an old word, but, if he wants to communicate his meaning, then he must explain such an unusual usage. Thus Alice, too, is correct. Whether he likes it or not, if Humpty Dumpty desires to communicate, he cannot arbitrarily create unique meanings for words, unless he informs his hearers/readers that he has done so.

The reason why New Testament scholars study Greek and Old Testament Hebrew (and Aramaic) is because the biblical writers wrote and willed their meaning under the norms of these languages. And the reason New Testament scholars study koine Greek rather than classical Greek is that the New Testament authors assumed that their readers knew and would interpret their works according to the Greek of their day, koine Greek, rather than the classical Greek language of earlier centuries.

Norms of the Utterance

The norms of the utterance is the specific meaning that the author has given to a word, phrase, sentence, and the like in a text.

Whereas a word or combination of words possesses a range of possible meanings within the norms of language, when an author uses a

Norms of Language   **Norms of Utterance**
Dictionary   Text

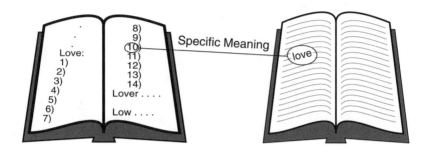

word in a text, it means only one thing. The task of interpretation is to discover this one specific meaning. In so doing the interpreter is seeking the norms of the utterance. Fortunately, the norms of language limit the number of possibilities, for we can assume that the author is interested in conveying his meaning to the reader. Because of this, the biblical author carefully remained within the norms of language in order to help his readers understand what he meant. Through the context the biblical author gives, he assists his reader in narrowing down the possible meanings to the one specific meaning.

Literary Genre

Literary genre refers to the literary form being used by the author and the rules governing that form.

In chapters 4 and following it will be pointed out that the biblical materials contain many different literary genres. The writers of the Bible sought to share their meaning. Thus, they worked within the literary conventions of their day that controlled the particular literary form they were using. Apart from a correct analysis of the literary form of a text and an application of the rules governing that genre, a correct understanding of the author's meaning is impossible. Beginning in chapter 5, we shall investigate the norms and conventions of several of the more important literary genres found in the Bible.

Bible and Genres

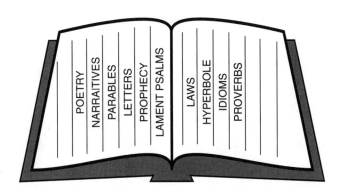

Context

Context refers to the willed meaning that an author gives to the literary materials surrounding his text.

The way an author helps his readers understand the meaning he seeks to convey is through context. It is quite common to hear people say such things as "The meaning of a passage is determined by the context," or "We know what Paul means here from the context." Yet what exactly is this context? If we say that the context of a text is the words, sentences, paragraphs, and chapters surrounding it, we may be attributing to such verbal symbols a meaning in and of themselves. Such a context possesses no more semantic autonomy than the text itself (see pp. 18–20), for such symbols cannot will a meaning. Apart from the willed meaning of the author, the verbal symbols that make up the context possess no meaning. It, like the text itself, is simply a collection of verbal symbols. Lacking personhood, such verbal symbols are inanimate symbols and cannot will a meaning. As a result, we must understand the literary context as consisting of what the author means by the shareable symbols he used before and after the text being investigated. Therefore, when we refer to the "context," we are referring to the shared pattern of meaning willed by the author in the words, sentences, paragraphs, and chapters surrounding the text. Thus, the context of Romans 3:20–21 is what Paul meant by the words that appear before Romans 3:20–21 and what he meant by the words that appear after Romans

3:20–21. Good authors, of course, seek to assist their readers by providing a context whose meaning will be easily understood.

A context is valuable because it assists the reader in understanding the meaning the author has given the text. It can do this because the author has willed a meaning to this context that aids in understanding the meaning of the text. The immediate literary context surrounding a text is the most valuable context available. Other literary contexts are of value to the degree that their authors thought like and used terms and grammar like the author. Social, political, and economic contexts are far less valuable. This is evident in that out of identical contexts a person may write as an anarchist or a monarchist, as a theist or an atheist, as a revolutionary or a loyalist, as a fatalist or a libertarian. What biblical writers believed, wished, and meant by their texts can only be known by the texts they have written and the literary contexts they have provided.

Great confusion can result if we do not pay careful attention to context. For instance, both Paul (Rom. 4:1–25) and James (2:14–26) use the term "faith" (*pistis*). Yet we will misunderstand both if we assume that by faith they mean "a body of beliefs." We will misunderstand Paul if we assume that he means "a mere mental assent to a fact," and we will misunderstand James if we assume that he means "a wholehearted trust." It is evident from the context that Paul means the latter (cf. Rom. 4:3, 5) and that James means the former (cf. 2:14, 19).

Questions

1. Define the following terms using your own words: meaning; implications; significance; subject matter; understanding; interpretation; mental acts; norms of language; norms of utterance; literary genre; and context.

2. How can an author "mean" something concerning things he knew nothing about?

3. How are "meaning" and "implication" alike? How are they different?

4. What is the difference between "interpretation" and "understanding"?

5. Do most sermons on the Gospels (or Acts, or Genesis to Esther) focus on the "meaning" or the "subject matter" of the text? Can you give an example?

6. Distinguish among the "specific willed meaning," the "pattern of meaning," and the "implications" of Paul's command "Greet one another with a holy kiss" (1 Cor. 16:20).

Exercise in Definition

(Which of the terms used in this chapter best describes the following?)

1. "What does Acts teach us in this chapter about the early church?"
2. "Oh, now I know what Paul meant!"
3. "Although Paul only told Timothy that women should dress modestly and not wear pearls (1 Tim. 2:9), he would probably also accept the view that women should not wear large amounts of any kind of expensive jewelry."
4. "What Paul means in Galatians 3:1–6 is that since the Galatians had received the Holy Spirit, the earnest of their salvation, by faith, therefore God had already accepted them and there was therefore no need for them to be circumcised."
5. "Evidently Paul was thinking of his past background as a Pharisee when he wrote this."
6. "This passage cannot mean what you are suggesting because the present participle in the text cannot be interpreted in this manner."
7. "What Jesus meant when he said 'Give to Caesar the things that belong to Caesar and to God the things that belong to God' is that you and I should obey our government and pay our taxes."
8. "This passage was not meant to be interpreted literally but figuratively."
9. "From Paul's use of the term elsewhere it is clear that it also means 'to declare righteous' here in Romans 3."
10. "Probably Moses was not thinking of this, but it seems to be applicable."
11. "Our text tells us that Jesus worked his first miracle at Cana of Galilee."
12. "What this passage tells us is that Jesus is also able to forgive our sins if we put our faith in him."

13. "The word Paul uses in this text can mean a number of different things."

14. "What we find in 1 Corinthians 15:3f. is an early church creed concerning the resurrection that Paul is quoting."

15. "What Paul said here is interesting, but I do not think that it has any value for us today."

16. "I was able to explain to Denise what the Bible means about being saved, but I was not able to persuade her to accept Christ into her heart."

3

Can Anyone Play This Game? The Spirit and Biblical Interpretation

Throughout the entire process of interpreting the Bible, the Holy Spirit is intimately involved. He was involved at the very beginning, as the cause of the inscripturation of the biblical materials. It was through his divine inspiration that the biblical authors wrote the Scriptures. He was involved in the recognition of which books were inspired and to be included in the New Testament (the development of the New Testament canon). The Spirit is also involved at the end of the interpretative process, as the believer seeks to apply the biblical teaching to his or her life.

The Role of the Spirit in Inspiration

The Bible is the product of divine inspiration (2 Tim. 3:16–17; 2 Pet. 1:20–21). As a result the Bible is the Word of God and reveals what Christians are to believe (matters of faith) and how they are to live (matters of practice). The terms "infallible" and more recently "inerrant" are often used to describe the reliability of the Bible. The former term focuses on the doctrinal reliability of the Bible; the latter on its factual reliability. It is not always understood, however, that these terms are essentially meaningless apart from an explanation of "what" is infallible and inerrant.

When Christians say that the Bible is infallible and/or inerrant, what does this mean? Does it mean that the spiritual or "existential" messages being taught in the Bible are true even if the accounts are not an accurate description of what took place, that is, that the accounts are not historical but "mythical"? Whereas certain existentialist interpreters might agree with this statement, this is not what Christianity has traditionally meant by these terms. Does it perhaps mean that the ethical (or "substructural") realities, lying beneath the plain or surface meaning of what the author meant, are true? Whereas some people (such as a "structuralist") might agree with this view, this, too, is not what Christianity has meant by these terms. Does it mean that the facts of the Bible are true? Yet what is a "fact" of Scripture?

We can resolve such confusion once we realize that the terms "infallible" and "inerrant" are judgments of propositions. They are evaluations of statements of meaning. Thus, the Christian claim that the Bible is infallible or inerrant means in essence that "what the authors of Scripture willed to convey by their words," their proposition or pattern of meaning, is true with regard to what they willed to convey. The term "infallibility" means that what the authors willed to convey with regard to matters of faith (doctrine) and practice (ethics) are true and will never lead us astray. The term "inerrant" means that what the authors willed to convey with regard to matters of fact (history, geography, science, etc.) are also true and will never lead us astray. What is determinative at all times, however, involves what the author, led by the Spirit, sought to convey by his text.

An illustration of this is found in Isaiah 11:12 where the prophet states that God "will gather the dispersed of Judah from the four corners of the earth" (RSV). What does he mean by this statement? Does he will to tell his readers, "I want you to know that the earth consists of four corners and God will bring his people back from these four corners"? Or does he will to tell his readers, "I want you to know that God will bring his people back from the ends of the earth"? (Notice how I use the expression "ends of the earth" in the preceding statement, even though I believe that the earth is round and has no "ends"!) If Isaiah meant to teach geography in this verse, then the verse is errant, not inerrant, because it would contain an error of geography. The earth has no "corners." However, if Isaiah did not will to teach geography, but wanted rather to teach the future regathering of God's people from throughout the world, then his statement can be infallible and inerrant.

The "what" of inspiration involves the Spirit's guiding the authors of Scripture as they wrote, as they willed to convey their pattern of meaning. As they wrote they were "carried along" (2 Pet. 1:21) by the Spirit, so that their writings are for the Christian the only infallible rule of faith and practice. Various passages reveal that this divine superintendence extends to the very words ("verbal symbols") used by the authors (cf. Matt. 5:18; Gal. 3:16). The question of "how" the Spirit guided the authors in their writing, however, is far from clear. At times he may have done this through a vision (Obad. 1; Nah. 1:1; Hab. 2:2; Rev. 1:11) or through a voice (Exod. 17:14; Jer. 30:1–2; 36:2; Rev. 1:11), but how Paul or Luke was guided by the Spirit in their writing is unclear. The style and theological emphases of the individual writers shine through their writings. This indicates that the Spirit worked with and through the personality of the human authors. As a result Christian theologians have seldom argued in favor of a dictation form of inspiration by the Spirit. Such explicit statements as Luke 1:1–4 also argue against such a view.

The Role of the Spirit in the Formation of the Bible

The process by which the sixty-six books that make up the Bible came to be collected and recognized as the Word of God involves the question of "canon." The term itself is a Greek word that referred to a staff or straight rod used as a means of measurement. The term soon came to mean a "rule" or "standard." In the history of the Christian church the term came to be used with respect to the books that were judged to be the "standard" by which the church should live.

In the process of recognizing which of the various books were part of the canon a number of factors played a role. It should be pointed out, however, that in this process the church did not "make" these books into the Word of God but merely "recognized" which books were in fact the Word of God. It was through the inspiration of the Holy Spirit that the books of the New Testament became the Word of God. Thus, the canon of the New Testament was "closed" when the last book of the New Testament was written. The recognition of which books were part of this New Testament, however, took time.

One of the factors that aided the church in recognizing which books were part of the New Testament canon was apostolic authorship or association with an apostle. Thus, the Pauline, Petrine, and Johannine epistles were assumed to be part of the canon due to their being apostolic. This was true also of the Gospels of Matthew and John. Luke–Acts was associated with Paul; Mark with Peter; and Hebrews with Paul as well. Another factor that played a role in the church's recognition of the canon of Scripture was antiquity and continuous usage throughout the church. Thus, those books that were written late and had a limited and local history of usage within the church were not recognized as canonical. Still another factor was the unity and agreement of these books with the rest of Scripture. The church rightly assumed that the Spirit who inspired such works as the Gospels and the Pauline letters could not have inspired works that contradicted them. (From this it is evident that they were able to "harmonize" Paul and James in a way that Luther was not.)

God's Superintendence and Spirit's Guidance

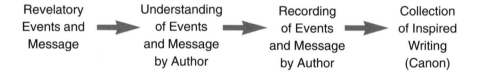

| Revelatory Events and Message | Understanding of Events and Message by Author | Recording of Events and Message by Author | Collection of Inspired Writing (Canon) |

Along with these, another important factor was the divine superintendence of this process by the Holy Spirit. Through his leading the church recognized which books belonged to the canon of Scripture. It is difficult for a Christian to assume that the God who sent his Son to be the Savior of the world would have in his providential rule of creation stopped at that point. The New Testament teaches that God through his Spirit then went on to inspire the recording and interpretation of that great redemptive event. Thus, not only the birth-life-death-resurrection of God's Son was sovereignly ruled over by God but also the interpretation and recording of that event. In the sovereign rule of God, the church was then led by the Spirit to recognize which of those books were divinely inspired and the infallible rule of faith and practice of the church. (This is true even if some of the church's reasoning was flawed in that not all New Testament books were written by apostles and many books of the Bible are anonymous.)

Although it cannot be "proven," it also seems reasonable to think that in his providential rule, God likewise saw to it that those inspired texts would not be lost or corrupted in any major way. When we compare the thousands of Greek manuscripts of the New Testament, the tens of thousands of early translations in Latin, Syriac, Coptic, and Arminian, and the thousands of lectionaries (church Scripture readings), it is not difficult to see in all this the work of the Spirit of God in making sure that the text of Scripture would not be lost but carefully preserved.

The Role of the Spirit in the Interpretation of the Bible

In the previous section we described how the Spirit was active in guiding the biblical writers in the process of inscripturation. As the writers chose the words and grammar by which they sought to express their meaning, they were led by the Spirit. Yet is the Spirit also active in guiding and aiding the reader in the process of interpretation? If so, where in the process does this take place? Is it in the "understanding" of the text's meaning? In discovering the various "implications"? In the evaluation of the text's meaning, in its "significance"? Is the Spirit involved in all these areas?

As Luther, Calvin, and the other Reformers reflected on how the Spirit was involved in the interpretation of Scripture, they spoke of the inward work of illumination and conviction of the Holy Spirit. This view is also expressed at times by saying that apart from the Spirit we cannot "fully" or "truly" understand the Bible. Using the terminology discussed in chapter 2, it would appear that what the Reformers called "illumination" refers to understanding the meaning of the text, "conviction" to the attribution of a positive significance to the text. In other words, the Spirit helps the reader understand the pattern of meaning that the author willed and convinces the reader as to the truth of that teaching.

Textual support for this view is frequently seen in 1 Corinthians 2:14 where Paul states, "The man without the Spirit does not accept the things that come from the Spirit of God, for they are foolishness to him, and he cannot understand them, because they are spiritually discerned." This is interpreted as meaning that, apart from the Spirit, a person cannot "understand" the meaning of biblical texts. Without the Spirit these texts are simply foolish riddles. Yet before we assume that Paul, and the English translators of Paul, are using the term "understand" in the exact

sense in which we defined the term in chapter 2, we must look more
closely at this verse.

What does Paul mean when he says that apart from the Spirit these
things are "foolishness"? Does he mean that a person without the Spirit
will not be able to come to a correct mental grasp of what the biblical
text means? Is Paul saying that apart from the Spirit the biblical teachings are incomprehensible?

The meaning of the term "foolishness" is best understood by observing how Paul uses it elsewhere. In 1 Corinthians 3:19 the term is used
as follows: "For the wisdom of this world is foolishness in God's sight."
Here, it should be noted, something is foolish to God! Clearly Paul
does not mean that God cannot arrive at a correct mental grasp of what
this world calls wisdom! God is omniscient; he understands everything.
God, of course, understands what this world calls wisdom. He rejects
it, however, as foolishness. The term "foolishness" in 1 Corinthians
3:19 refers not to what we have called "understanding" but rather to
"significance." God understands perfectly well what this world calls wisdom, but he critiques it. He evaluates it. He condemns it as foolishness. In 1 Corinthians 1:20 the verbal form of this word is used, and
Paul states similarly, "Has not God made foolish the wisdom of the
world?" Here (1:20), in the chapter before 1 Corinthians 2:14, as well
as in the chapter following (3:19), Paul uses the expression "foolish"
to refer to the significance God attributes to something (this world's
wisdom).

Should this same meaning be attributed to the term in 1 Corinthians 2:14? It would appear so, for what Paul is saying is not that unbelievers cannot arrive at a correct mental grasp of the things of the Spirit.
They can and do, but they attribute to this understanding of the author's
meaning a negative significance. They reject it as "foolishness." Thus,
in the first three chapters of 1 Corinthians we have the following parallel. The unbelieving world can understand the things of the Spirit,
what the biblical text means, but it rejects what it understands as foolishness. Similarly, God understands the wisdom of this world, but
rejects it as foolishness. In both instances there is a correct mental grasp
of what is meant (understanding) followed by a rejection of its value
(significance).

In a similar way it would appear that the terms for "understand" in
1 Corinthians 2:12 and 14 are best understood as meaning something
different than acquiring a correct mental grasp of meaning. It refers

rather to embracing as true these biblical truths. It is probably best to see the terms "does not accept," "foolishness," and "cannot understand" as referring to various ways in which the unbeliever critiques the divine revelation. This critique (significance) is based on an understanding of that message. The understanding of the text is rejected in several different ways: (1) it is not accepted, not received eagerly or welcomed, because it is opposed to human wisdom (cf. 1 Cor. 1:18–25); (2) it is judged as foolishness because it conflicts with their sense of truth; and (3) it is not believed as being true because only the Spirit can convince us of the truth of the gospel message. It would appear that whereas 1 Corinthians 2:14 refers to the work of the Spirit in "conviction" or "significance," it does not deny but rather assumes that an unbeliever can "understand" the gospel message.

Can a person apart from the Spirit understand the Bible? Let us for a moment assume that we are able to form two groups of college students with equal intelligence, background, and dedication to making good grades. One group consists of Christians, the other of non-Christians. They are assigned this task: Describe in eight to ten pages what Paul meant by Romans 3:20–21. Would their grades be sufficiently different? Would Christians be able to understand and then interpret their understanding in ways that would cause them to receive a higher grade than the non-Christian group? Would the Spirit assist the Christians in obtaining a correct mental grasp of the meaning and thus enable them to obtain better grades? (It might be argued that Christians would have an advantage because of greater familiarity with the Bible, but it might also be that they would also possess a disadvantage in that they might bring with them numerous misunderstandings as well. What teacher of the Scriptures in college or seminary has not encountered strange interpretations that some Christian students bring with them to school!)

I would suggest that the curve of grades for both groups, all other things being equal, would be quite similar. Non-Christians can arrive at a correct mental grasp of the meaning of the Bible. They can understand the Scriptures. Otherwise why try to explain the gospel message to them? Why would Paul reason every Sabbath in the synagogues (Acts 18:4)? Why would he seek to explain the gospel message (17:2–3) and seek to persuade (19:8–9)? Why would someone today seek to explain the "four spiritual laws" unless he or she were convinced that the listener was capable of understanding these laws? A Christian apologetic and defense of the faith to unbelievers is based on the assumption that they are capable of understanding the teachings of Scripture.

Where then does the work of the Spirit come into play? Could it be in revealing the "implications" of the author's pattern of meaning? Certainly the Christian has far greater desire to understand such implications than a non-Christian. This may be true, but is a non-Christian capable of understanding the implications of the meaning of a biblical text? Again let us imagine that the same two groups of students are asked to write an eight- to ten-page paper on modern-day implications of Jesus' words in Matthew 6:24, "No one can serve two masters. Either he will hate the one and love the other, or he will be devoted to the one and despise the other. You cannot serve both God and Money." Would there be any major difference in the grading of these two groups of papers? Assuming the same intelligence and dedication to grades, this is unlikely. (If it is assumed that the Christians will work with greater devotion on their papers because of their love for God, it is unfortunate but probably true that the non-Christians' devotion to grades may be every bit as great as the devotion of some Christians to God!)

There are several important consequences that arise from the universal ability that people possess to understand the meaning of a biblical text. The first is that Christians can study the works of non-Christians with great profit. It is simply not true to claim that only believers can understand biblical teachings. If by "understand" we mean "to possess a correct mental grasp of the meaning of the text," it is quite apparent that evangelical Christians do not have a corner on understanding the Bible. I must confess that I have frequently learned more from reading the works of nonevangelicals than those of evangelicals. When I went to seminary the best texts and commentaries were written by scholars who made no claim to be evangelical Christians. There were not many well-researched, scholarly works available that were evangelical in nature. Today this has changed significantly. Evangelical scholarship has made remarkable progress in recent years, and some of the very best texts available today have been written by evangelicals. Yet it must still be admitted that many of the very best works in biblical studies are being written by those who make no claim to be evangelical Christians. Even without the Spirit, they are able to describe accurately and well what the authors of Scripture meant in their texts, and we can benefit from their labors.

One point that has not been dealt with up to this point is the problem of sin and how this affects the ability of humans to understand the biblical teaching. How do the fall and the resulting depravity of humanity affect the ability of people to understand divine revelation? Have they affected the reasoning ability of humanity so as to require a divine enabling to counter and overcome the results of sin? Without minimizing the effect of the fall, we must also guard against exaggerating its effect as well. The image of God has been tarnished and corrupted but not destroyed. It has been corrupted but not lost (James 3:9). Part of that image involves the ability to reason, which is central to interpretation. It is apparent that the ability to understand what an ancient author meant (whether biblical or nonbiblical is not important at this point) has not been lost. We can understand the writings of other people. We can also understand the meaning the biblical writers sought to share. Sin may cause us not to want to accept/believe what they say, but this involves significance and not understanding. Furthermore, the result of sin on the reasoning process of humans affects both Christians and non-Christians. There is nothing in Scripture that tells us that the regenerating work of the Spirit transforms the mental abilities of people. What it does affect is our value systems, the significance we attribute to the meaning of biblical texts.

If we recognize that anyone with normal intelligence can obtain a correct mental grasp of the meaning of Scripture, then is the ability of all humans to understand this the work of the Spirit? To understand the illumination of the Spirit in this manner, however, would be simply to equate it with human intelligence. This reduces the illumination of the Spirit to the ability of humans to reason and still does not resolve the issue, for it does not explain what the Spirit provides for the believer that he does not provide for the unbeliever.

A Concluding Illustration

The role of the Spirit in biblical interpretation can perhaps best be described by means of an illustration. At the annual lectureship on biblical studies at the Interpretation School of Theology, Ludwig Kopfwissen of Wissenheim University delivered an address entitled "Paul's Doctrine of Justification by Faith." In this one-hour lecture Kopfwissen described, more clearly than anyone else has ever done before, what Paul meant by his doctrine of justification by faith. He also carefully and brilliantly described the implications of this doctrine in the life of the Christian church both past and present. If the Apostle Paul had been present, he might even have said, "Thank you, Professor Kopfwis-

sen. No one has ever explained what I meant as clearly and as well."
After he is warmly applauded, however, the professor adds, "Aber Sie
wissen doch dass es ganz Humbug ist—But you know, of course, that
this is all nonsense!"

After the address someone happens to see the wife of Professor
Kopfwissen, who is a committed Christian, and asks her, "Frau (Mrs.)
Professor, what do you think Paul meant by his doctrine of justification
by faith?" To this she replies, "You must understand that my training
is not in theology but in chemistry, but I guess"—and at this point tears
begin to form in her eyes—"I guess, Paul meant that God has done
everything for us!"

Who understands Paul's teaching better? The professor or his wife?
The issue, of course, depends upon what is meant by "understands."
If, as defined in chapter 2, it means a correct mental grasp of Paul's
meaning, it is clear that Professor Ludwig Kopfwissen "understands"
Paul better. He has a far greater grasp of the pattern of meaning willed
by the apostle. But, as in 1 Corinthians 2:14, it is foolishness to him,
because he has not been convicted/convinced by the Spirit of its truth.
He cannot appreciate it, because such conviction comes from the Spirit.
On the other hand, Frau Kopfwissen appreciates the meaning of Paul's
teaching. She, too, understands, although not nearly as completely,
what Paul meant, but through the Spirit she accepts this as the wisdom
of God.

What, then, are the implications of this for the study of the Bible?
There are several. For one, the role of the Spirit in interpretation is not
an excuse for laziness. All the prayer in the world cannot substitute for
a Bible dictionary, if we do not know the meaning of a biblical word.
For understanding the biblical text, meditation is no replacement for
looking up how the author uses such terms elsewhere in his writings.
The goal of acquiring a correct mental grasp of the author's meaning
is not achieved by personal piety. To pray that the Spirit would help us
understand the meaning of a text because we do not want to spend time
studying the text or using the tools that have been made available to us
(such as commentaries, concordances, dictionaries, etc.) may border
on blasphemy, for it seeks to "use" the Spirit for our own ends. The
Holy Spirit brings to the believer a blessed assurance of the truthfulness of the biblical teachings, but he cannot be manipulated to cover
for laziness in the study of the Word of God.

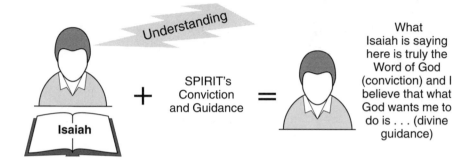

On the other hand, to pray that the Spirit would help us recognize the truth of the text (its significance) or to show which of the implications apply particularly to us and our situation (divine guidance) is both highly appropriate and devout. For what does it profit a study of the Bible, if we understand its meaning perfectly, but never submit to its teaching and obey its implications for our lives!

Questions

1. How would you respond at a Bible study or in a Sunday school class when two people say, "The Holy Spirit has shown me that the text means . . . ," and these two supposedly "Spirit-given" interpretations are contradictory?
2. Can a person understand the "four spiritual laws" and not be a Christian?
3. Can a person understand the meaning of John 3:16 and not be a Christian? Can he or she understand the truthfulness of John 3:16 and not be a Christian?
4. Do you know a person who "understands" the meaning of John 3:16 but is not a Christian?
5. What advantage does a Christian have over a non-Christian in the study of the Bible?
6. Explain what Paul meant in 1 Corinthians 2:14 in your own words.
7. Besides "conviction" what else does the Spirit do in "conversion"?

Different Games in the Same Book: Different Forms of Scripture

Within the Bible, as within literature in general, there exist two main kinds of language: "referential language" and "commissive language." When we use referential language, the main goal is to pass on information. This form of language seeks to describe. It seeks to be nonemotional in nature. It seeks to pass on facts. In our society such language is becoming more and more important, for it is the language of science. Physicists, chemists, biologists, engineers, computer technicians, and medical doctors use this form of language when seeking to communicate with one another. It is also the language of philosophers, automobile mechanics, dentists, and tire salesmen. It is the advice we receive in hardware stores, lumber yards, cooking recipes, and word processing seminars.

Commissive language, on the other hand, has as its main goal evoking decisions, conveying emotions, eliciting feelings, and arousing the emotions. It is the language of poets, people in love, college football coaches, lieutenants leading men in battle, motivational speakers, and speakers at high school graduations. Whereas referential language appeals to the "mind," commissive language appeals to the "heart." The former is more cognitive in its aim; the latter, more emotive. The difference can be seen most easily when we compare different kinds of literature. We read an automobile manual in a different way than we read a love letter. The description of "0.016 inch gap" for a spark plug is interpreted as meaning that we should leave a 0.016 inch gap for each spark plug! The description of missing a sweetheart so much that our heart aches, that we cannot sleep, that our heart stops beating, is interpreted quite differently. Automobile repair manuals are meant to be taken literally, and are referential in nature. Love letters are not. They are to be interpreted figuratively, metaphorically, for they are commissive in nature. If we interpret repair manuals figuratively and love letters literally, disaster, or at least a lack of communication, will result.

It should not be concluded from what has been said that referential language cannot convey emotions or that commissive language cannot convey information. A physician may use referential language to convey a diagnosis. The description "inoperable melanoma of the pancreas" is primarily referential in nature, but the meaning it conveys, "incurable cancer," is nevertheless extremely emotive. Some information by its very nature will elicit feelings. We can read the most sterile, objective description of the history of the Auschwitz death camp, and, despite the referential nature of the account, it will affect our feelings and emotions. Similarly, a love letter, despite its commissive nature, nevertheless conveys information. It reveals the love of the letter writer for the reader! As a result the terms "referential" and "commissive" are not exclusive in nature. They reflect rather the primary purpose of the language being used.

The descriptions "referential" and "commissive" extend not only to different kinds of literary forms, but also to the very words used within those forms. Note how various terms used in the abortion debates are frequently intended to convey not just information but emotions: fetus—unborn baby; pro-choice—pro-life; abort—murder; control of reproductive organs—killing one's baby. Compare also: prostitute—call girl—lady of the night—whore. Or: the biblical account—the biblical story—the biblical myth—what took place. Smart advertisers, preachers, and propagandists are well aware of how the choice of the right word can affect people. In this respect the terms "pro-life" and "pro-choice" must be labeled quite successful. They are stirring and emotive terms.

Playing by the Rules—Meaning and Literary Forms

It is obvious that our choice of words may at times be motivated less by a desire to inform and enlighten than by a desire to arouse and affect the emotions and will of the reader. The biblical writers were, of course, well aware of this and consciously chose to use words and literary forms that would best convey their meaning. At times they sought primarily to convey certain information (Luke 1:4). They then used those referential forms and terms that were best suited to convey this information. When they sought to convey the divine laws, they would use certain legal forms such as found in Exodus, Leviticus, Numbers, and Deuteronomy. At times the best form available to share certain information was that of a letter or epistle. Thus we find in the Bible various letters such as those of Paul, Peter, and John. At other times the narrative form was used to share information that was primarily historical in nature. Much of the Bible is made up of such material (Genesis through Esther, Matthew through Acts). Even in the prophetic literature we find narrative in Jeremiah 26–29, 32–45, 52; Haggai 1–2; Daniel 1–6.

Other forms of literature tend to be more commissive in nature. In such a category we would certainly place the Psalms and the Song of Solomon. It should also be noted that within much of the narrative materials we also find poetry (Exod. 15; Judg. 5; 1 Sam. 2; Jesus' use of poetry in the Gospels) and emotive sayings. Some biblical literature tends to contain elements of both kinds of language. Proverbs and prophecy are examples of this.

It is clear that there are various kinds of literary forms in the Bible. Each of them possesses its own rules of interpretation. The authors in using these literary forms consciously submitted themselves to the rules governing these forms in order to share their meaning with their readers. Each author assumed that his readers would interpret his words according to the rules governing that literary form. If we are not aware of the rules under which the biblical author wrote, misinterpretation almost certainly will take place. Think for a moment of a European soccer fan attending his first football and basketball games. In football the offensive and defensive players can use their hands to push their opponents. In basketball and soccer they cannot. In basketball players cannot kick the ball, but they can hold it with their hands. In soccer the reverse is true. In football everyone can hold the ball with their hands but only one person can kick it. In soccer everyone can kick the ball but

The Rules of the Game

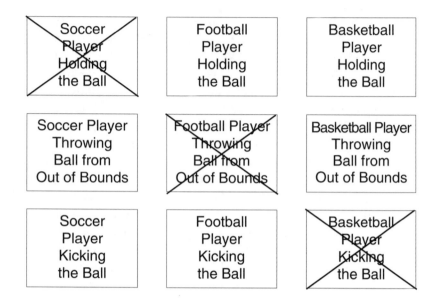

only one person can hold it. Unless we understand the rules under which the game is played, what is taking place is bound to be misinterpreted.

In a similar way there are different "game" rules involved in the interpretation of the different kinds of biblical literature. The author has played his "game," has sought to convey his meaning, under the rules covering the particular literary form he used. Unless we know those rules, we will almost certainly misinterpret his meaning. If we interpret a parable (Luke 16:19–31) as if it were narrative, or if we interpret poetry (Judg. 5) as if it were narrative, we will err. Similarly, if we interpret a narrative such as the resurrection of Jesus (Matt. 28:1–10) as a parable, we will also err (1 Cor. 15:12–19).

A good example of the importance of this occurred in my own life as a young Christian. I did not like reading the Beatitudes. Whenever I read them I became depressed, for they always left me feeling guilty and wondering whether I was truly a Christian. The reason for this was that I misunderstood their literary form. I read them as being "conditions for membership" in the kingdom of God. As a result when I read, "Blessed are the poor in spirit, for theirs is the kingdom of heaven. . . . Blessed are the meek, for they will inherit the earth" (Matt.

5:3, 5), I felt condemned, because I knew that I was not as poor in spirit as I ought to be. There was still too much pride and arrogance in my life. Furthermore, I was not one who could turn the other cheek easily (Matt. 5:39). Similarly, when I read, "Blessed are those who hunger and thirst for righteousness, for they will be filled" (Matt. 5:6), I realized that I did not long for God's righteousness as I should. The result was again feelings of guilt and depression.

As time went on, however, I began to wonder if my guess as to the literary form of the Beatitudes, and as a result my understanding of the rules governing its interpretation, were incorrect. Are the Beatitudes to be interpreted as "conditions for membership" in the kingdom of God? Or are they instead to be understood as "blessings pronounced upon those who are already citizens of the kingdom"? In other words, are the Beatitudes to be understood as entrance requirements for salvation or as ascriptions of praise and congratulations to those who already possess salvation? It became evident that rather than being entrance requirements, the Beatitudes are to be understood as blessings pronounced upon those already within the kingdom. This is evident for several reasons. For one, the audience to whom these Beatitudes was delivered was the disciples (Matt. 5:1–2; Luke 6:20). Thus, they cannot be conditions for discipleship in that they were addressed to those who already were disciples. Second, the closest analogies to the Beatitudes are the words of comfort addressed to God's people in such places as Isaiah 29:19; 49:13; and especially 61:1–2. Third, the grammatical form of the Beatitudes is not conditional in nature. There is no, "*If* you become poor in spirit, you will inherit the kingdom of heaven." Rather the grammatical form is that of a pronouncement. Finally, the fact that Matthew 5:3 and 10 both end with "for theirs is the kingdom of heaven" indicates that the Evangelist understood everything in Matthew 5:3–10 as dealing with the same basic theme. As a result they must be interpreted as blessings pronounced upon God's people, those who are either "persecuted because of righteousness" (Matt. 5:10) or may in the future be persecuted because of their faith.

In my earliest attempts to understand the Beatitudes I was playing under the wrong "game" rules. I misinterpreted the particular literary form with which I was dealing. Thus, a correct understanding of the meaning was impossible. And it would have remained impossible, unless I changed my expectation of the kind of game, literary form, which I was playing. I was applying soccer rules when I was really playing basketball; I was using the rules on how to interpret entrance requirements for pronouncements of blessings. Yet this did not make a correct interpretation hopeless. It was always possible to start over and change to another generic expectation, from soccer to basketball, from entrance requirements to pronouncements of blessing. When I approached the Beatitudes with a new and correct expectation appropriate to this literary form, understanding was possible, for I now shared the rules of interpretation associated with this literary form with Jesus and Matthew.

Today I find encouragement and strength from these congratulatory words of blessing. Thus, when I was asked if there was a passage of Scripture I wanted read at my father's funeral, one of the passages I chose was the Beatitudes. When the pastor then read, "Blessed are those who mourn, for they will be comforted," I was able to understand that these were divine words of blessing and comfort addressed by God to us who mourned the death of our beloved Christian father and husband. God was promising us that there was coming a day of great comfort when "There will be no more death or mourning or crying or pain" (Rev. 21:4), a day of joyous reunion (1 Thess. 4:14).

In the following chapters we will look at the rules governing various forms of biblical literature. Since we want to understand what the author meant when he wrote, that is, the pattern of meaning he willed to convey, we need to know the rules he followed when he wrote. Knowing that the writers of Scripture willingly submitted themselves to the norms of language governing those literary forms, we will be better able to understand what they wrote, if we know what those norms are. Thus, in the following chapters we will look at the norms of language involved in proverbs; prophecy; poetry; idioms; hyperbole; parables; biblical narrative; epistles; covenants; laws and commandments; and psalms.

Questions

1. Have you ever misinterpreted something because you were interpreting it by the wrong set of rules? (For example, what is "traveling" in college basketball? In pro-basketball? I once saw a friend strike out in slow-pitch softball because he thought the rules were the same as in fast-pitch softball. He thought you received three

strikes, as in fast-pitch softball, whereas in our game of slow-pitch you received only two.)

2. Why does the difference between "referential" and "commissive" language not require a change in the definition of "meaning" given in chapter 2?

3. Does an incorrect understanding of the literary form of a text mean that we will never be able to grasp the meaning of that text?

Part 2

The Specific Rules
for the Individual
Games

5

The Game of Wisdom —Proverbs

A proverb is a short pithy saying, frequently using metaphorical language, which expresses a general truth. Proverbs are sometimes called "maxims" or "aphorisms." Proverbs are found throughout the Bible. Best known, of course, is the book called "Proverbs," but major parts of the books of Job, Ecclesiastes, and James consist of proverbs. The proverb was a popular form of Jesus' teachings and examples are found throughout the Gospels. They are also found scattered throughout the rest of the Bible (Ps. 49:16–20; Isa. 5:21; Jer. 23:28b; 31:29; etc.).

One of the best known proverbs is found in Proverbs 22:6: "Train a child in the way he should go, and when he is old he will not turn from it." Not too long ago I heard of a pastor who told his congregation after reading this verse, "I know that my children will follow the Lord, because I am training them up in the way they should go." As a father I am thankful to God that my three children are committed Christians. Yet it would be the height of folly and ignorance to claim that they are committed Christians because their father trained them perfectly in the way they should go. On the contrary, it is because of God's grace that they have followed the Lord. And, all too often, this has been despite the inconsistencies and failures of their father. Second, such a public statement places children under a terrible burden. If they do choose to serve the

Lord, this is now to be credited to their father's godliness. Only if they choose not to serve the Lord, can they manifest their own individuality! More important still, however, is the fact that this reveals an incorrect understanding of what a proverb is and how it should be interpreted.

Is a proverb to be interpreted as a universal law? Is it like the law of the Medes and the Persians, which could never be overruled (Esther 8:8)? Is it to be interpreted absolutely, like the laws of thermodynamics, which describe what must always take place? It is apparent when reading proverbs that many of them seem to be less than absolute in their applicability:

- "but whoever listens to me [wisdom] will live in safety and be at ease, without fear of harm" (Prov. 1:33; cf. also 2:8). (Do not some believers experience suffering and even martyrdom because of their faithfulness to God?)

- "Honor the LORD with your wealth, with the firstfruits of all your crops; then your barns will be filled to overflowing, and your vats will brim over with new wine" (Prov. 3:9–10). (Does "tithing" insure farmers of being wealthy and successful? Note how in 15:16–17; 19:22; 28:16 the writer knows that faithfulness does not always result in prosperity. Cf. also from the Apocrypha, Tobit 3:21.)

- "The LORD does not let the righteous go hungry but he thwarts the craving of the wicked. Lazy hands make a man poor, but diligent hands bring wealth" (Prov. 10:3–4). (Is all poverty due to laziness?)

- "Misfortune pursues the sinner, but prosperity is the reward of the righteous" (Prov. 13:21). (Is prosperity a measure of piety? Are there no pious poor? Are all rich people devout? Cf. Luke 6:20.)

- "A wise servant will rule over a disgraceful son, and will share the inheritance as one of the brothers" (Prov. 17:2). (How often do "servants" share the inheritance equally with the children?)

- "He who oppresses the poor to increase his wealth and he who gives gifts to the rich—both come to poverty" (Prov. 22:16). (Do not some people become quite wealthy by their oppression of the poor?)

- "For all who draw the sword will die by the sword" (Matt. 26:52; cf. also Prov. 15:1; Matt. 6:21; Luke 16:10; etc.). (Some mercenaries seem to do quite well with the sword!)

It is clear that these proverbs cannot be considered absolute laws, because there are exceptions to them. They are, of course, true in general. (Would many people in Germany in June 1945 disagree with the general truth of Matt. 26:52?)

Proverbs are not "laws." They are not even "promises." They are general observations learned from a wise and careful look at life. Such observation is not limited to the Bible but is found throughout ancient Near Eastern, Greek, and Egyptian literature, as well as in most present-day cultures. Yet the biblical proverbs have an added dimension to them. They have been formulated not simply by observing "life," but by observing life in the light of divine revelation. Thus, the biblical proverbs reveal not just the best of human wisdom but that wisdom fil-

The Making of a Biblical Proverb

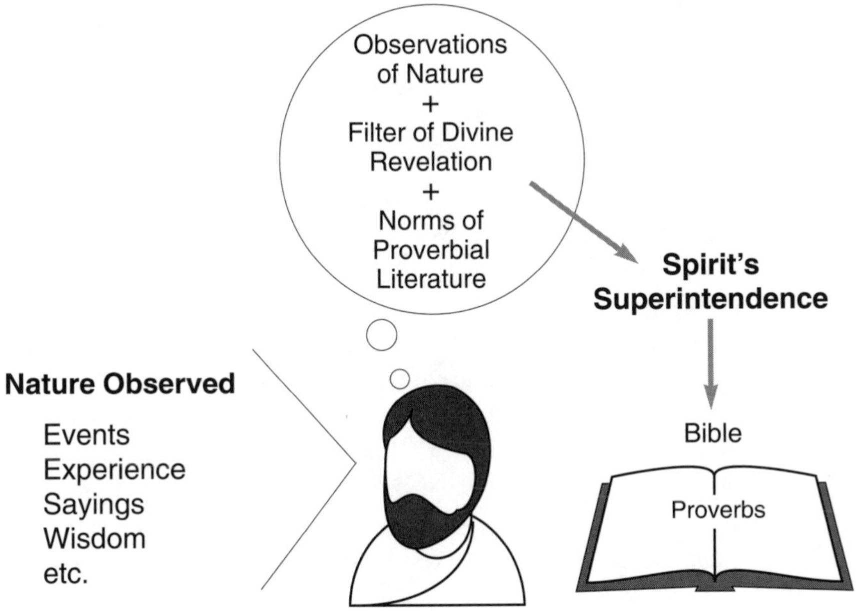

Observations
of Nature
+
Filter of Divine
Revelation
+
Norms of
Proverbial
Literature

**Spirit's
Superintendence**

Nature Observed

Events
Experience
Sayings
Wisdom
etc.

Bible

Proverbs

tered through the revelation of Scripture and recorded under the direction of the Spirit.

A proverb is a short, pithy saying that expresses a wise, general truth concerning life. A biblical proverb is a short, pithy saying that expresses a wise, general truth concerning life from a divine perspective. Because of the "general" nature of proverbs, there is present the possibility of exceptions. The existence of such exceptions in no way refutes the truth of the proverb, for what the proverb says is true in the majority of instances. Thus, the fact that godly parents who train their children in the way they should go at times have ungodly children does not refute this proverb. In the great majority of instances the result is indeed children who desire to follow in the faith of their parents.

We cannot understand the Book of Job without realizing that this piece of wisdom literature wrestles with this very problem. Job is a devout man whose world has fallen apart. His "comforters" are well versed in the proverbs found in the wisdom literature of their time. Their error is that they assume that these proverbs are absolute laws without exceptions. As a result, they believe that the tragedies Job has experienced must be due to his ungodliness. Note how they throw various proverbs at him. After his wealth, his children, and health have been taken from him, they say:

- "Consider now: Who, being innocent, has ever perished? Where were the upright ever destroyed? As I have observed, those who plow evil and those who sow trouble reap it." (4:7–8)
- "He saves the needy from the sword in their mouth; he saves them from the clutches of the powerful." (5:15)
- "Does God pervert justice? Does the Almighty pervert what is right? When your children sinned against him, he gave them over to the penalty of their sin. But if you will look to God and plead with the Almighty, if you are pure and upright, even now he will rouse himself on your behalf and restore you to your rightful place." (8:3–6; cf. also 11:13–20; 18:5–21; etc.)

In the case of Job, however, these proverbs do not fit. He is an exception. His misfortunes are not due to his sin. Thus, he cannot repent of any specific guilt that would have caused them. He is an exception to such proverbs as, "When a man's ways are pleasing to the LORD, he makes even his enemies live at peace with him" (Prov. 16:7; cf. also 10:9, 15, 29; 11:6; 12:7, 21; 13:21; etc.).

In interpreting this form of literature, therefore, we must be aware of the fact that a proverb functions as a general truth. The presence of exceptions does not refute the truth of a proverb. Of course, some proverbs can be universal in scope, but a proverb need not be universal, as long as it involves observations of what generally happens in life. These wise and memorable observations, which are usually found in poetic form, provide inspired principles upon which believers can and should build their lives.

Thus, even if Proverbs 22:6 cannot be absolutized into a universal law, it nevertheless reveals a great truth that should encourage Christians to rear their children in the "fear and admonition" of the Lord. The fact that such children more often than not follow in footsteps of their parents should motivate us to do so with great dedication. In my own experience I have not ceased being impressed when I encounter second- and third-generation pastors, missionaries, and dedicated laypeople who witness to the truth of this proverb. Of course, there are exceptions. The writer of Proverbs was no doubt aware of Eli's sons who did not follow in the paths of their devout father, and of people who did not follow in the ways of their godly parents (cf. the kings of Judah who were good and did right in the eyes of the Lord in 2 Chron. 14ff. and how some were followed by evil sons). Nevertheless at times these exceptions, like the prodigal son, "come to their senses" (Luke 15:17; cf. the case of Manasseh in 2 Chron. 33:12) and return home to the faith of their parents. The authors of the biblical proverbs wanted their readers to interpret them as general truths and to understand the meaning he willed to convey through them.

Questions

1. Can you find a biblical proverb, one not given in this chapter, which as a general rule is true but has exceptions?
2. Can you think of some present-day proverbs that we willingly accept even though there are exceptions?
3. Make up a proverb.
4. What kind of poetry is found in Proverbs 10–17? (See chapter 7.)

6

The Game
of Prediction—Prophecy

For many people prophecy is a synonym for prediction. As a result, the prophetic books of the Bible are frequently thought of simply as long lists of predictions concerning future events. Yet when we read the prophetic literature, it is evident that a great portion, if not the greatest portion, of these books, consists of narrative and proclamation. This aspect of prophecy is also evident from the fact that within the Old Testament canon, the books of Joshua through 2 Kings are called the Former Prophets. This further reveals that a prophet was understood more as a *forth*teller of the divine message than a *fore*teller of future events. His ministry was often more concerned with proclamation than prediction. (Even my English dictionary under "prophecy" lists as its first meaning "To reveal the will or message of God" and as its second meaning "To predict the future"!)

In this chapter we shall look, however, at the predictive dimension of prophecy. Such prophecy is found throughout the Bible, from Genesis (cf. 3:15; 12:2–3; 27:39–40; 49:1–28) to, of course, Revelation. There are major sections of the Gospels that are devoted to prophetic prediction (Matt. 24–25; Mark 13; Luke 13:28–35; 21:5–36; etc.). Frequently a distinction is made between "prophecy" and "apocalyptic." The former is usually associated with "this"-worldly events, whereas the latter is associated with "other"-worldly events. Such a distinction, however, is overly simplistic, for, as we shall see, prophecy frequently uses cosmic terminology in its depiction of "this"-worldly future events. In this chapter we shall not distinguish between prophecy and apocalyptic.

Within this literary genre we encounter certain assumptions ("game rules") that the authors thought their readers shared. The prophets expected that their readers would interpret their prophecies according to the rules associated with this literary form. Unfortunately, some of these rules are not clear to us today, and this causes serious difficulties in interpreting this kind of literature.

Judgment Prophecies

One of the rules of prophetic literature, and one that most readers of the Bible are unaware of, involves prophecies of judgment. An example of this is found in Jonah 3:4 where the prophet proclaims to the city of Nineveh, "Forty more days and Nineveh will be overturned." When the city hears this message, the people "from the greatest to the least, put on sackcloth" (v. 5) and the king himself decrees a time of mourning and repentance. We then read, "When God saw what they did and how they turned from their evil ways, he had compassion and did not bring upon them the destruction he had threatened" (v. 10). But what of Jonah's prophecy? Does the lack of divine judgment make Jonah a false prophet?

Not at all, for Jonah, and both the hearers and readers of this prophecy, knew something about judgment prophecies of which most modern-day readers are not aware. This rule concerning judgment prophecies, shared by Jonah, the Ninevites, and the original readers of this Book, is found in Jeremiah 18:7–8: "If at any time I [the Lord] announce that a nation or kingdom is to be uprooted, torn down and destroyed, and if that nation I warned repents of its evil, then I will relent and not inflict on it the disaster I had planned." Similarly, "if at another time I announce that a nation or kingdom is to be built up and planted, and if it does evil in my sight and does not obey me, then I will reconsider the good I had intended to do for it" (vv. 9–10; cf. Ezek. 33:13–15).

Another example of this rule is found in Micah 3:12 where the prophet states, "Therefore because of you, Zion will be plowed like a field, Jerusalem will become a heap of rubble, the temple hill a mound overgrown with thickets." In Jeremiah 26:16–19 this prophecy is quoted and its lack of fulfillment noted. Micah was not considered a false prophet, however. The prophecy was not fulfilled because the king and the people feared the Lord and sought his favor (v. 19). Thus, God relented of the judgment that was prophesied. Still another example of a judgment prophecy that was averted is found in 1 Kings 21:20–29.

The rule shared by Jonah and his hearers (and the biblical author and readers) is that judgment prophecies are conditional. Jonah knew this. This was why he fled from the Lord. If Jonah had been commissioned to preach a prophecy of judgment upon Nineveh that was irreversible, he would gladly have gone to Nineveh. He would have run to Nineveh to preach such a message! Oh how wonderful it would have been for him to have preached to the people of Nineveh that God's judgment was about to fall upon them and that there was no way of escape! How joyously he would have proclaimed such a message of damnation and destruction on this evil kingdom.

But Jonah knew that if he preached this prophecy, there was a possibility that the Ninevites would repent and thus be spared of the divine judgment. This possibility Jonah feared and dreaded. Jonah wanted these brutal Nazis of his day to be damned. He wanted them destroyed, and he knew that any judgment prophecy always presumed that such judgment would be avoided if the people repented. This is evident from what we read in Jonah 4:1–2: "But Jonah was greatly displeased and became angry. He prayed to the LORD, 'O LORD, is this not what I said when I was still at home? This is why I was so quick to flee to Tarshish. I knew that you are a gracious and compassionate God, slow to anger and abounding in love, a God who relents from sending calamity.'" One of the rules that the prophetic writers shared with their readers is that judgment prophecies always assume that, if the hearers repent, the judgment will not take place. This was part of the "norms of language" involving judgment prophecies.

The Language of Prophecy

Another aspect of prophecy with which the interpreter must reckon involves the vocabulary used by the prophetic writers. Much of the terminology found in prophecy makes use of customary imagery used in this genre. For instance, in the judgment prophecy found in Isaiah 13:9–11 we read:

> See, the day of the LORD is coming—a cruel day, with wrath and fierce anger—to make the land desolate and destroy the sinners within it. The stars of heaven and their constellations will not show their light. The rising sun will be darkened and the moon will not give its light. I will punish the world for its evil, the wicked for their sins. I will put an end to the arrogance of the haughty and will humble the pride of the ruthless.

Because of the cosmic imagery found in this prophecy, many interpreters assume that it is referring to the end of history. Yet it is clear from Isaiah 13:1 ("An oracle concerning Babylon that Isaiah son of Amoz saw") and 19 ("Babylon, the jewel of kingdoms, the glory of the Babylonians' pride, will be overthrown by God like Sodom and Gomorrah") that the prophecy concerns the Babylonian empire of the sixth century B.C. The Babylonian kingdom that destroyed Jerusalem and the Solomonic temple, this empire that sent the cream of Judean society into exile, was about to experience divine judgment.

Yet this judgment is described in cosmic terminology. Such terminology, however, was part of the imagery and symbolism available to the prophets when they sought to describe God's intervention in history and his sovereign rule over the kingdoms of this world (cf. Dan. 2:21; 4:17, 25, 34–35; 5:21). Such imagery was not meant to be interpreted literally. The sun was not actually going to be darkened; the moon would not stop giving its light; the stars would not stop showing their light. "What" the author willed to communicate by this imagery, that God was going to bring judgment upon Babylon, was to be understood "literally." And that willed meaning, God's judgment upon Babylon, did take place. This prophecy was fulfilled with the rise and rule of the Persian empire over the territories once ruled by Babylon, and the later readers of this prophecy knew that this prophecy had indeed been fulfilled. Babylon had been judged just as the prophecy proclaimed, and it was God's doing just as the cosmic imagery described. The imagery, itself, however, was understood by the prophet and his audience as part of the stock terminology used in this kind of literature to describe God's intervention into history.

In Acts 2:14–21 Peter and Luke interpreted the events of Pentecost in a similar way as they saw in it the fulfillment of the prophetic message of Joel:

Then Peter stood up with the Eleven, raised his voice and addressed the crowd: "Fellow Jews and all of you who live in Jerusalem, let me explain this to you; listen carefully to what I say. These men are not drunk, as you suppose. It's only nine in the morning! No, this is what was spoken by the prophet Joel: 'In the last days, God says, I will pour out my Spirit on all people. Your sons and daughters will prophesy, your young men will see visions, your old men will dream dreams. Even on my servants, both men and women, I will pour out my Spirit in those days, and they will prophesy. I will show wonders in the heaven above and signs on the earth below, blood and fire and billows of smoke. The sun will be turned to darkness and the moon to blood before the coming of the great and glorious day of the Lord. And everyone who calls on the name of the Lord will be saved.'"

These cosmic signs did not literally take place at Pentecost, even though what the author willed to convey by those signs did. God did enter into history and bring about the fulfillment of the prophecy of Joel. God in fulfillment of his promises gave to the church the blessed gift of the new covenant. The kingdom had come in its firstfruits, for the Spirit came upon every believer. The conventional cosmic imagery used in this prophecy of Joel was understood by both Peter and Luke as being fulfilled in the events of Pentecost.

There have been attempts to deny that the prophecy of Joel 2:28–32 was fulfilled at Pentecost. Usually this is due to a misunderstanding of the figurative nature of this cosmic terminology. Some have suggested that Luke and Peter believed that Pentecost was "kind of like" what Joel prophesied but not its actual fulfillment. Such a manipulative interpretation of this passage of Acts, however, is impossible in light of Peter's words in Acts 2:16: "this is what was spoken by the prophet Joel." Furthermore such interpretative gymnastics are unnecessary when we are willing to accept what the author meant by the use of such terminology. We need only note other passages to see how widespread the use of such cosmic terminology is in the Bible (Isa. 24:23; Jer. 4:28; 13:16; 15:9; Ezek. 32:7–8; Joel 2:10, 31; 3:15; Amos 8:9; Hab. 3:11; Matt. 24:29; Mark 13:24–25; Luke 21:25; Rev. 6:12). (Attempts to see Mark 15:33; Matt. 27:45; Luke 23:44–45 as the fulfillment of this prophecy also err. They do not explain the signs of Acts 2:19 and most of 2:20. Second, and more important, they err because Peter and Luke associate the fulfillment of these signs with what is happening then and there on the day of Pentecost.)

The Figurative Nature of Prophetic Language

A clear example of a "nonliteral" prophecy is found in Isaiah 11:6–9 and 35:8–10. In describing the peace and security of the messianic age the author writes in chapter 11,

> The wolf will live with the lamb, the leopard will lie down with the goat, the calf and the lion and the yearling together; and a little child will lead them. The cow will feed with the bear, their young will lie down together, and the lion will eat straw like the ox. The infant will play near the hole of the cobra, and the young child put his hand into the viper's nest. They will neither harm nor destroy on all my holy mountain, for the earth will be full of the knowledge of the LORD as the waters cover the sea.

Yet later in chapter 35 he writes,

> And a highway will be there; it will be called the Way of Holiness. The unclean will not journey on it; it will be for those who walk in that Way; wicked fools will not go about on it. No lion will be there, nor will any ferocious beast get up on it; they will not be found there. But only the redeemed will walk there, and the ransomed of the LORD will return. They will enter Zion with singing; everlasting joy will crown their heads. Gladness and joy will overtake them, and sorrow and sighing will flee away.

In reading these two passages it is evident that we have a problem if we interpret the imagery literally. In the first passage wild beasts are present in the messianic age, living peaceably with the rest of creation. In the second wild beasts are not present. Yet there is no contradiction in the mind of the author. The author of Isaiah 35 knew what was written in Isaiah 11. In his mind they did not contradict each other. On the contrary, the willed meaning of these two figurative scenes is identical. In the messianic kingdom there is peace and security. The metaphorical language in which this is described may be different (wild animals living peaceably or no wild animals being present), but what the author sought to convey by this imagery is the same. There will be no more war, no more fighting, no more hostility. There will be peace! We must not confuse the metaphorical nature of the language the prophet uses with the meaning he wills by that language. The context he provides by having both these passages in his work helps his readers understand the meaning of each passage.

Another example is found in Luke 3:4–6: "A voice of one calling in the desert, 'Prepare the way for the Lord, make straight paths for him.

Every valley shall be filled in, every mountain and hill made low. The crooked roads shall become straight, and rough ways smooth. And all mankind will see God's salvation.'" This summary of the message of John the Baptist, which comes from Isaiah 40:3–5, is found in each of the Gospels (Mark 1:3; Matt. 3:3; John 1:23). Only Luke, however, adds Isaiah 40:4, which refers to the valleys being filled in, the mountains and hills being made low, the crooked roads becoming straight, and the rough places being made smooth. If these are to be interpreted literally, this would require major geographical and topographical changes on this planet. But Luke makes no mention of such physical changes accompanying the ministry of John the Baptist. This imagery is furthermore found in the intertestamental literature: "For God has ordered that every high mountain and the everlasting hills be made low and the valleys filled up, to make level ground, so that Israel may walk safely in the glory of God" (Baruch 5:7); "And the high mountains shall be shaken, and the high hills shall be made low, and shall melt like wax before the flame" (Enoch 1:6). It is clear that Luke understood this imagery figuratively as referring to the humbling of the proud and the exaltation of the repentant through the preaching of John the Baptist. (Cf. Luke 14:11 and 18:14, where the term "made low" means "to humble.")

Still another example of the figurative nature of prophetic terminology is found in the description of the New Jerusalem in Revelation 21. The walls of the city are described as 144 (note the symbolism: 144 = 12 x 12; cf. also 7:4–8; 21:12) cubits thick (v. 17), approximately two hundred feet thick! The thickness of these walls are meant to indicate the safety and security of the New Jerusalem. Who could break through walls so strong and thick? Yet we also read that the gates of the city are never shut (v. 25). What good are walls if the gates are left open? And since the gates of a city were the weakest part of a city's defense system, why would someone want twelve gates (v. 12)? Once again the prophet has used different metaphors, which at first glance look contradictory, to describe the security and safety of the New Jerusalem. Thick walls reveal safety, but so do the gates (and their number) being opened all the time. The meaning of this figurative language is clear. The believer will not need to worry, for there is peace and security in the New Jerusalem. (For other examples of figurative terminology in prophecy, compare: Isa. 3:24–4:1; 34:1–17; Jer. 4:23–31; 15:8–9; Nah. 1:4–5; Hab. 1:6–9; Mark 13:14–16.)

The Making of a Biblical Prophecy

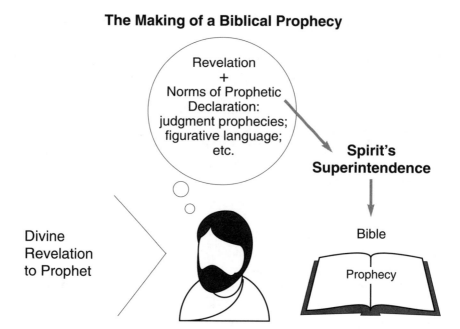

The *Sensus Plenoir* or "Fuller" Meaning of the Text

There are times when a prophetic text appears to have a fulfillment other than what the prophet himself apparently expected. (The following are frequently given as examples: Matt. 1:22–23; 2:15, 17–18; John 12:15; 1 Cor. 10:3–4.) Is it possible that a prophecy may have a deeper meaning or "fuller" sense than the prophet envisioned? According to this view, whereas the prophet willed to convey one truth, God had a different truth he willed to convey by the same vocabulary and grammar. If we assume for the sake of argument that this does in fact occur, this fuller meaning or *sensus plenoir* can never be known until after the fact. The willed meaning of the prophet is accessible to the reader because of the context the author has provided. We know the prophet's vocabulary, style, and grammar, and this literary context enables us to understand what he willed to convey by his prophecy. But what about the alleged fuller meaning of God? How can we know this? The literary context does not help, for we have no access to God's vocabulary, style, and grammar but only the prophet's!

Two other difficulties are connected with such a view. The first involves how we today can discover a fuller, divine meaning in a text of which the divinely inspired author was ignorant. It seems arrogant, to say the least, to assume that our knowledge is sufficiently greater than that of the inspired prophets that we can know something about their words of which they were totally unaware. Two errors seem to be at work here. The one demeans divine inspiration, the other elevates human reason to the extent that the latter is greater than the former! (We cannot help but think here of those who claim to possess such a "fuller" understanding of the return of the Son of God that they can predict the time of his coming, when the Son of God, himself, claimed that he did not know this [Mark 13:32].)

The other difficulty with this view is that proof of such a fuller meaning could only be demonstrated by examples that are after the fact, that is, they would only be known after this alleged fuller revelation has taken place. Before the fulfillment of this deeper meaning, no one understood the *sensus plenoir*. From a pragmatic point of view, since we can only perceive such a deeper fulfillment after the fact, seeking such deeper meanings is of little value. At its best it is purely speculative and a waste of energy. We cannot know with certainty such a future, deeper meaning.

Rather than appealing to a "fuller sense" distinct and different from that of the biblical author, however, it may be wiser to see if the supposed *sensus plenoir* is in reality an implication of the author's conscious meaning. Thus, when Paul in 1 Corinthians 9:9 quotes Deuteronomy 25:4 ("do not muzzle an ox while it is treading out the grain") as a justification for ministers of the gospel living off the gospel, this is not a "fuller" meaning of the text unrelated to what the author sought to convey. Rather, it is a legitimate implication of the willed pattern of meaning contained in Deuteronomy 25:4. If as a principle animals should be allowed to share in the benefits of their work, how much more should the "animal" who is made in the image of God and proclaims the Word of God be allowed to share in the benefits of that work! Thus, what Paul is saying is not a fuller and different meaning from what the writer of Deuteronomy meant. On the contrary, although this specific implication was unknown to him, it is part of his conscious and willed pattern of meaning. Perhaps such prophecies as Matthew 1:22–23 and 2:15 are best understood as revealing implications of the original prophecies in Isaiah 7:14 and Hosea 11:1. Whereas in Isaiah's day the prophet meant that a maiden would give birth to a son who was named "Immanuel," that willed meaning also allows for a virgin one day to give birth to a son who would be Immanuel. Whereas God showed his covenantal faithfulness by leading his "Son," his children, back from Egypt to the promised land in Moses' day so also did he lead his "Son," Jesus, back from Egypt to the promised land.

Concluding Remarks

As a young Christian I was taught to approach the prophecies of the Bible as if they were photographic portraits of future events. They were to be understood as divine camera shots of what was one day to take place. As time progressed, however, I became aware of the figurative language used by the prophets. As a result, I would suggest a different, perhaps better analogy.

There is considerable difference between the art of the fifteenth and sixteenth centuries and that of the nineteenth century. Fifteenth- and sixteenth-century art is realistic in nature and seeks to reproduce objects in a way similar to how a photographer does today. A scene in the paintings of that day shows the buttons people have on their clothing clearly, even if they are standing in the distance. Everything is painted in exact detail. A magnifying glass held over small sections of the painting reveals amazing detail. It almost seems that the painter possessed microscopic brushes in order to paint with such precision. On the other hand, at the end of the nineteenth century artists tended to be more impressionistic than realistic in their paintings. Such paintings often appear to be only globs of paint. You have to stand back and observe the overall painting in order to understand what the author is seeking to convey. I would suggest that the ancient prophets "painted" their prophetic message more along the lines of such nineteenth-century impressionists as Monet and Renoir than in the manner of the Flemish and Italian schools of the fifteenth and sixteenth centuries.

In the interpretation of prophetic literature we must remember that meaning is determined by the author. The author in turn sought to share that divinely revealed meaning by means of this particular literary form. In doing so he submitted himself to the rules governing this form of literature, which were known to him and his readers/hearers. If we want to understand his willed meaning, we must know those rules and interpret his work within the historical and literary context of his day. If we tear his prophecy out of this context and neglect those rules, we will never understand the meaning of such literature, the author's willed meaning. Instead, we will treat his prophetic message as predictive inkblots into which we will pour our own meanings. As a result the prophetic message will no longer be a "word from God's inspired prophet" but rather a "word from a confused reader." We shall then be "teaching as doctrines the precepts of men" (Mark 7:7 RSV).

When we interpret various prophecies within their historical contexts, it is evident that what was a future prediction "then" (when the prophet wrote) may no longer be a future prediction "now" (when we read the prophecy). Numerous prophetic predictions have already found their fulfillment in such events as the fall of Jerusalem (Jeremiah; Ezekiel); the judgment of such nations as Samaria (Hosea; Amos; Micah), Babylon (Isa. 13–14, 21, 47; Jer. 50–51; Daniel), Edom (Obadiah), Moab (Isa. 15–16), Damascus (Isa. 17), Ethiopia (Isa. 18), Egypt (Isa. 19), Tyre (Isa. 23), Nineveh (Nahum; Zeph. 2), Philistia (Zeph. 2); the return of the Jews from Babylonian exile (Isa. 40–66; Jer. 30–33; Ezek. 40–48; Mic. 4–5; Haggai; Zechariah); the birth, ministry, death, and resurrection of Jesus Christ (Isa. 4, 7, 9, 11, 40, 53; Jer. 23, 33; Mic. 5; Zech. 3); the coming of the Spirit at Pentecost (Jer. 31; Joel 2). There are others that still await fulfillment such as the coming of a great tribulation (Matt. 13; Mark 24; 2 Thess. 2); the glorious appearing of the Son of Man (Matt. 24; Mark 13; 1 Thess. 4; 2 Thess. 2); and the final judgment (Matt. 25; Rev. 20). By seeking to understand the willed meaning of the author for the situation in which he wrote, we shall be able to avoid interpreting certain prophecies that have already been fulfilled, such as the return of the Jews from Babylonian exile, as having had a present-day fulfillment or as still awaiting a future fulfillment.

Questions

1. Unlike Jonah's prophecy against Nineveh, there are judgment prophecies in the Bible that did take place and the prophet knew that they would. Does this refute what we have said about judgment prophecies in this chapter?

2. Read Mark 13:12–27. Is any of the terminology used in this portion of Scripture "figurative"? Is any of it "literal"? On what basis should we decide this?

3. What is the difference between "*fore*telling" and "*forth*telling"?

4. Are most of the Old Testament prophecies in Isaiah, Jeremiah, and Ezekiel already fulfilled or still to be fulfilled? How do we decide this?

7

The Game
of Rhythm—Poetry

One of the literary forms found most frequently in the Bible is poetry. What distinguishes biblical poetry from prose is not so much any one single feature as much as a combination of them. Clearly the most important feature is "parallelism" or rhythmic balance between different lines. Another feature is "terseness." In poetry the lines of sentences tend to be much shorter in comparison to the lines found in prose. The lines also tend to be of "equal length," whereas in prose there is great variety in the size of sentences. Poetry also tends to be "disinclined to use conjunctions and particles." (In a recent study it was pointed out that Hebrew prose tends to use the sign of the direct object [*ʾet*], the relative pronoun [*ʾaser*], and the definite article [*ha*] six to eight times more than Hebrew poetry.) On the other hand poetry is far more inclined to use "figurative language."

Poetry was not clearly distinguished from prose in older translations such as the King James Version, but in modern translations such as the New International Version, Revised Standard Version, and New English Bible the poetic sections of the Bible are clearly seen. If we skim through the more historical books of the Old Testament, from Genesis to 2 Chronicles, we find that most of the material in these books appears as solid paragraphs, as prose. On the other hand, if we skim through Job, Psalms, Proverbs, Isaiah, and the other prophets, we will find that much, if not most, of the material in these books appears in broken lines, as poetry. The solid black typifies the prose sections of Scripture; the poetic sections contain much more "white" space and the black is quite broken. Yet even in the prose sections of the Bible, we find major sections of poetry (see Gen. 3:14–19; 4:23–24; 49; Exod. 15; Deut. 32–33; Judges 5).

Poetry Compared to Prose

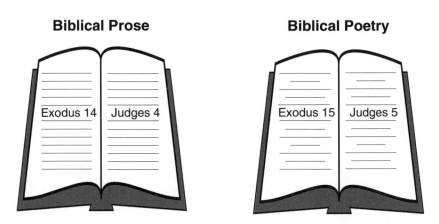

The use of poetry in ancient times, as in our own, indicates that the writer is less concerned with precise description or scientific accuracy than with evoking emotions and creating certain impressions. Poetry is clearly "commissive" rather than "referential" in nature (see pp. 73–74). Physicians do not use poetry to describe their patients' medical problems, but lovers do when they seek to express their love for each other. The biblical poets and song writers frequently used this form in their praise and adoration of God. When they did so, however, they anticipated that their readers would interpret what they wrote according to the rules governing such poetry. We are fortunate that in the Bible we have at least two places where prose and poetic accounts of the same event appear side by side. In comparing them we can see that they function in different ways, although in each instance they still convey what the author meant by the verbal symbols he placed in these different literary genres.

In the fourth chapter of Judges the author describes in prose form the defeat of the Canaanite commander, Sisera, by the Israelite tribes of

Naphtali and Zebulun. The forces of Israel are led by the prophetess Deborah and the reluctant Barak. The battle is described in the straightforward manner of a historical narrative in verses 12–16, as is the death of Sisera in verses 17–22. A historical summary concludes the account in verses 23–24. In chapter 5 it is obvious, however, that the account is quite different. The solid black prose of chapter 4 has given way to the broken, uneven "white" space of chapter 5. This indicates that chapter 5 consists of poetry. The writer even tells us this in verse 1 when he states, "On that day Deborah and Barak son of Abinoam *sang this song.*"

When we compare the poetic description of the battle in chapter 5 with that of chapter 4, we notice several differences. We read, for example, in 5:4–5:

> O LORD, when you went out from Seir,
> when you marched from the land of Edom,
> the earth shook, the heavens poured, the clouds poured down water.
> The mountains quaked before the LORD, the One of Sinai,
> before the LORD, the God of Israel.

Here, in contrast to chapter 4, we read that when God led his people into battle "the earth shook" and "the mountains quaked." In the past some commentaries interpreted this literally and referred to earthquakes having been involved in the defeat of Sisera and his army. But it is interesting to note that no reference to earthquakes is found in the prose description of the battle in chapter 4. In poetry and song how can the author describe to his reader that the people were led in battle by the Lord? It is by saying that when God led his people against Sisera, "the earth shook before them." "The mountains quaked" in fear when God led the people of Israel into battle. This is how the poet has described the victory God gave his people over their enemies. We should not interpret this literally, however, for this is the language of poetry. As poetry it seeks to elicit an emotive response of joy rather than to impart information about the technicalities of the battle.

We also find in 5:19–20 the following description:

> Kings came, they fought;
> the kings of Canaan fought at Taanach by the waters of Megiddo,
> but they carried off no silver, no plunder.
> From the heavens the stars fought,
> from their courses they fought against Sisera.

Again it is interesting to note that in the past, before the poetic nature of much of the Old Testament was recognized, commentaries often interpreted "From the heavens the stars fought" as indicating that God sent meteor showers upon the Canaanite army (as in Josh. 10:11) and helped defeat them in this manner. Yet we have no hint of this in the prose description of the battle in chapter 4. It only appears in the poetic song celebrating this victory in chapter 5! This should cause us to question whether the author wanted his readers to interpret this literally. It appears more likely that he was seeking to describe in song what happened when Israel went into battle. God was with them, giving courage to his people and instilling fear in their enemies. This the poet describes by stating that the stars of heaven (and, of course, the *God* of the stars of heaven) fought on behalf of the people of Israel.

A final illustration of the poetic nature of chapter 5 can be seen by comparing the description of the death of Sisera in 5:24–30 with that in 4:17–22. In the earlier account the author portrays Sisera as fleeing on foot (4:17), explains why he trusted Jael (v. 17), how Jael greeted Sisera (v. 18), how Sisera was thirsty (v. 19), and that Sisera was asleep from exhaustion when Jael drove a tent peg through his temple (v. 21). Nothing of this is "sung" in chapter 5. On the contrary, the synonymous parallelism found in verses 25, 26, and 27 is not concerned with a careful explanation of what happened. It seeks rather to sing about the defeat of Israel's dreaded enemy:

> She struck Sisera, she crushed his head,
> she shattered and pierced his temple.
> At her feet he sank,
> he fell; there he lay.
> At her feet he sank, he fell,
> where he sank, there he fell—dead. (Judges 5:26c–27)

Another example in which we find a poetic account standing side by side with a prose account of the same event is found in Exodus 14 and 15. Once again it is obvious that chapter 14 is prose because of its solid black paragraphs; chapter 15 is clearly poetry because of the unevenness of its paragraphs and the amount of "white space." The writer also makes this clear by his introduction: "Then Moses and the Israelites *sang this song* to the LORD" (v. 1). Thus we have in chapter 14 a description of the Lord's victory over the army of Pharaoh in the form of prose, and in chapter 15 that victory is described in poetry.

We find in the poetic version of this victory several descriptions that cannot be taken literally:

> I will sing to the LORD, for he is highly exalted.
> The horse and its rider he has hurled into the sea. (v. 1)

> Pharaoh's chariots and his army he has hurled into the sea.
> The best of Pharaoh's officers are drowned in the Red Sea. (v. 4)

> In the greatness of your majesty you threw down those who opposed
>   you.
> You unleashed your burning anger; it consumed them like stubble.
>   (v. 7)

> By the blast of your nostrils the water piled up.
> The surging waters stood firm like a wall;
> the deep waters congealed in the heart of the sea. (v. 8)

> You stretched out your right hand and the earth swallowed them. (v. 12)

> Sing to the LORD, for he is highly exalted.
> The horse and its rider he has hurled into the sea. (v. 21)

It is clear that in the above we possess a highly metaphorical description of how God delivered his people from the army of Pharaoh. In verses 1, 4, and 21 God is depicted as a mighty warrior who picks up in his hands the forces of Pharaoh and throws them into the Red Sea. Yet in chapter 14 the forces of Pharaoh are described as having followed the people of Israel into the Red Sea, so that when the waters returned to their normal position the Egyptians drowned. We also find in verse 7 a rather awkward description of God's destruction of the Egyptian forces. They are "consumed . . . like stubble." Yet Pharaoh's forces were not "burned" but "drowned"! This, however, poses no problem for the writer, because the expression "consumed . . . like stubble" is a common metaphor for judgment and destruction (cf. Isa. 5:24; 47:14; Joel 2:5; Obad. 18; Nah. 1:10), and God brought judgment that day upon Pharaoh's army. (For an example within poetry itself of literal and picturesque descriptions of the same event standing side by side, compare 2 Sam. 22:1–4 with 22:7–20, and Ps. 18:1–3 with 18:6–15.)

In Colossians 1:15–20 we have an example of New Testament poetry that is quite troubling. For some reason the poetic character of this passage is not delineated in the English translations, but it is the Nestle-Aland edition of the Greek New Testament. The poetic parallelism is seen most clearly as follows:

A *He is the* image *of the* invisible God, *the firstborn* over all creation (1:15).

A¹ And *he is the* head *of the* body, the church; he is the beginning and *the firstborn* from among the dead, so that in everything he might have the supremacy (1:18).

B *For by [in] him* all things were created; things in heaven and on earth, visible and invisible, whether thrones or powers or rulers or authorities (1:16);

B¹ *For* God was pleased to have all his fullness dwell *in him* . . . (1:19)

C *all things* were created *by [through] him* and *for him;* He is before all things, and in him all things hold together. And he is the head of the body, the church; he is the beginning and the firstborn from among the dead, so that in everything he might have the supremacy (1:16d–18).

C¹ and *through him* to reconcile *to himself all things,* whether things on earth or things in heaven, by making peace through his blood, shed on the cross (1:20).

The parallelism of the above is more clear in the Greek text than in translation.

The difficulty in interpreting this passage is due to 1:20. At first glance this verse appears to teach universalism, that in the end all people will be saved (reconciled). Now the problem evangelical Christians have with this verse and this interpretation is not that they do not want to be universalists. On the contrary, we all have friends and relatives who are not believers, and no Christian wants to think that these friends and relatives will perish eternally. Thus, I would always vote a "universalist ballot" in this respect. The problem is that the fate of unbelieving people will not be decided by how Christians vote! Heaven is not a democracy. God does not act by majority vote. The fate of unbelieving people is decided by the will of God, and God has revealed elsewhere in numerous places that, when people die without having repented and having put their faith in Jesus Christ, the result is eternal separation from God, hell. The basic problem with this passage is that it appears to conflict with what Paul and the Scriptures clearly teach elsewhere (Rom 2:6–10; 1 Thess. 5:9; 2 Thess. 1:9; etc.).

There have been a number of ways in which this conflict has been explained. One of the most common is to understand the universal reconciliation of 1:20 in terms of Colossians 2:15 and Philippians 2:10–11. A serious hostility exists between God and "all things," and the "reconciliation" that takes place involves a reluctant submission of those opposed to God to his lordship. It is the kind of peace that comes about by God crushing Satan (Rom. 16:20). Thus, the reconciliation of all things that takes place involves not a serene and blissful peace in which animosity and opposition come to an end. Rather, it is a reconciliation in which all enemies and opposition come under the rule of God and must acknowledge his lordship. In his rule and lordship, however, God judges and damns the unrighteous to eternal judgment.

Perhaps a better way of interpreting 1:20, however, is to take into consideration the poetic nature of this passage. It is interesting to note that the word "all" is used eight times in the Greek text. This is not surprising in light of the fact that in the Jewish and Greek literature of Paul's day, the term "all" appears with unusual frequency in statements describing God's role in creation. The poetic nature of the passage and the use of "all" in literary statements dealing with creation should caution us against demanding a literal interpretation of this term. "Poetic license" might require its use in this passage even if the author did not want the term to be interpreted literally. We should also note the poetic balance between the following:

> *all things (ta panta)* were created *by him (di' autou)* and *for him (eis auton)* (1:16d)

> and *through him (di' autou)* to reconcile *to himself (eis auton)* *all things (ta panta)* (1:20a)

In light of this poetic parallelism, we need to be careful not to press this language too literally. Colossians 1:15–20 is best understood as a joyous, poetic statement (it may even be a song) that celebrates the creative and redemptive work of Jesus as the Redeemer and Lord of all creation. We should not demand of it a literal scientific accuracy any more than we require it of the great Christmas hymn when we sing

> Hail the heav'n-born Prince of Peace!
> Hail the Sun of Righteousness!
> Light and life *to all* He brings [Note: not "offers" but "brings"]
> Ris'n with healing in His wings.

The meaning of Colossians 1:15–20 is what Paul meant when he wrote it. But in writing this, he accepted its poetic nature. Thus, his use of "all" should not be pushed. What Paul meant to reveal in this poem is that Jesus Christ is divine, that he is the one who is to inherit the rule of the world (he is the "firstborn"), that he is the one through whom the world was created, that he existed before all things, that he is the ruler of the church and its redeemer, and that it is through his sacrificial death that God has brought about reconciliation with the church. To press this literary form and require that each of these statements be interpreted literally in each instance, however, is to violate the norms of language involving poetry under which the apostle worked.

Specific Forms of Poetry

Usually when we think of what makes a poem, two things come to mind. A poem possesses rhyme and rhythm. Both are found in the following nursery rhyme:

> Mary had a little lamb.
> Its fleece was white as snow,
> and everywhere that Mary went
> the lamb was sure to go.

Rhyme is present in the words "snow" and "go." The second and fourth lines have a similar rhythm of six beats. Rhythm is even more essential for poetry than rhyme. In a similar way what is essential to biblical poetry is "parallelism." (For examples of rhyme in poetry, see Isa. 5:7 and 33:22 in the Hebrew text.) This means that the lines of Hebrew poetry have a similar cadence or rhythm. The original term used to describe this parallelism was "parallelismus membrorum." (Robert Lowth coined this expression to describe Hebrew poetry in 1753, and his work was written in Latin.) This rhythmic parallelism can occur in different forms. (The appropriateness of the following designations is debated, but they are traditional and none of the alternative designations has won universal approval.)

Synonymous Parallelism

In this kind of parallelism the various lines express a thought that is similar to what has preceded. It may strengthen or develop that thought. Sometimes the same thought is repeated, as in the following:

> Ask and it will be given to you;
> seek and you will find;
> knock and the door will be opened to you.
> For everyone who asks receives;
> he who seeks finds;
> and to him who knocks, the door will be opened. (Matt. 7:7–8)

> hallowed be your name,
> your kingdom come,
> your will be done
>   on earth as it is in heaven. (Matt. 6:9c–10)

In the first example we have three parallel lines that for all intents and purposes repeat the same thought. To "ask," to "seek," and to "knock" are simply different ways of saying the same thing. They are synonyms for praying. They do not denote different kinds or intensities of prayer. Similarly, to "have it given," to "find it," to "have it opened," and to "receive it" are just different ways of saying "God will answer your prayers." (The use of passive verbs allowed the devout Jew to avoid using God's name and thus avoid the danger of using the name of God in vain.)

In the second example, which comes from the Lord's Prayer, we again have a threefold repetition of the same essential thought. When God answers any of the three lines, the same event will take place. Jesus will return, and history as we know it will come to its conclusion. Only then will God's name be "hallowed on earth as it is in heaven," "his kingdom come on earth as it is in heaven," and "his will be done on earth as it is in heaven." Thus, the Lord's Prayer is repeating the same longing that the early church expressed when it prayed,

Marana tha, "Come, O Lord." (1 Cor. 16:22; Rev. 22:20)

Love your enemies,
do good to those who hate you,
bless those who curse you,
pray for those who mistreat you. (Luke 6:27–28)

In this example we again have a repetition of similar thoughts, but in the first instance we have the more general teaching "Love your enemies," whereas in the following three lines we may have specific examples of how that love is to be manifested. We have another example of this in Mark 3:4 when Jesus asks, "Which is lawful on the Sabbath: to do good or to do evil, to save life or to kill?" From the first general thought (do good—do evil) we proceed to a more specific application (save life—kill).

In synonymous parallelism the number of lines varies. There must, of course, be at least two (which is the most common; see Isa. 54:1a, b [Gal. 4:27a, b]; Mark 3:24–25; 8:18; Rom. 11:33), but there are also examples of three (Ps. 100:1–2; Isa. 51:11; Jer. 9:23; Hos. 5:1; Amos 8:10; Mic. 1:7; Mark 9:43–48; Luke 23:29; 1 Cor. 13:1–3) and even four parallel lines (Jer. 2:8; 4:23–26; 5:17; Luke 6:29–30, 37–38; 17:27; Mark 13:24–25; Matt. 10:35). If we know that a saying involves synonymous parallelism, then we are able to deduce a helpful interpretive principle from this. Each line in such examples must be asserting the same or a related truth. Thus, if in the Lord's Prayer we are uncertain about what it means to pray for God's name to be hallowed, we are assisted in understanding this by realizing that this request is similar to praying that God send his kingdom. From the rest of the Gospels we know what the latter means. The kingdom of God, which has already arrived in part in the coming of Jesus and the Spirit, still awaits its glorious consummation. To pray for the consummation of the kingdom means to pray for God to bring history to a close and to establish his glorious reign upon the earth. Thus, we know, because of the synonymous parallelism, that the other two "thou petitions"—for the name of God to be hallowed and his will to be done—must deal with a similar thought. These three petitions pray for something far beyond what God can do in our own hearts, in the life of the people with whom we worship, and even in the life of Christendom in general. It looks forward to that great day when every knee will bow and every tongue confess that Jesus Christ is Lord to the glory of God the Father (Phil.

2:10–11). Thus, by knowing the literary form we are able to go from the known member of the parallelism to the unknown.

Similarly, if I want to know what it means to love my enemies, I can find insight and help from the other parallel members of Luke 6:27–28. By knowing that these four lines are an example of synonymous parallelism, we are able to understand the less clear from the more clear. To love our enemies means to do certain loving acts. The four parallel lines do not speak of emotions. They speak of the Christian doing loving acts of kindness toward his or her enemies. This is why Jesus can command his followers to love their enemies. We cannot command the emotions. We cannot command people to "emote" or "feel" toward their enemies. We can, however, appeal to a person to do loving acts of kindness.

Antithetical Parallelism

In this form of poetry, the second line contrasts with the first. Instead of providing a synonymous parallel or a specific example of the general content found in the first line, it provides an antithetical statement. This is the most common form of parallelism in the Bible. In Jesus' teachings alone we have over 130 examples. In Proverbs there are entire chapters that are devoted to this literary form (10–15). Some examples are:

Better a meal of vegetables where there is love
than a fattened calf with hatred. (Prov. 15:17)

A wise son brings joy to his father,
but a foolish son grief to his mother. (Prov. 10:1)

Likewise every good tree bears good fruit,
but a bad tree bears bad fruit.
A good tree cannot bear bad fruit,
and a bad tree cannot bear good fruit. (Matt. 7:17–18)

Whoever can be trusted with very little can also be trusted with much,
and whoever is dishonest with very little will also be dishonest with much.
    (Luke 16:10)

Whoever acknowledges me before men, I will also acknowledge him
    before my Father in heaven.
But whoever disowns me before men, I will disown him before my Father
    in heaven. (Matt. 10:32–33)

Whereas in synonymous parallelism we frequently find examples that are three or four lines long, because of its very nature antithetical parallelism is usually limited to two lines. This is seen in the above examples, although in the third example we have an instance in which the first two and the last two lines are also an example of antithetical parallelism.

In interpreting this literary form we should note again that if we understand any of the two statements making up the example, this will help us understand the other. It should also be remembered that in interpreting antithetical parallelism we are dealing with poetry and not prose. We need to allow for the possibility of poetic license. Thus, if what we find seems to conflict at first glance with what the same author or another biblical writer says elsewhere, we should take note of the poetic nature of the passage.

Step of Climactic Parallelism

In this form of parallelism the second line picks up the thought of the first line. However, instead of repeating that thought or giving an example as in synonymous parallelism, it advances the thought an additional step. As a result, although the two thoughts are related, the second raises the first to a higher level and brings it to a kind of climax. This form does not occur as frequently in the Bible, but some examples are as follows.

He who receives you receives me,
and he who receives me receives the one who sent me (Matt. 10:40).

Do not think that I have come to abolish the Law or the Prophets;
I have not come to abolish them but to fulfill them (Matt. 5:17).

In the first example we can see a clear advance of the first statement by the second. The one who receives a disciple is in fact receiving Jesus, and in turn the one who receives Jesus receives none other than God himself. The second example reveals that far from coming in order to do away with the Old Testament (the Law and the Prophets), Jesus came not just to keep them, but to bring them to their fulfillment. For

Matthew this means not only Jesus' fulfillment of the prophetic promises
by his sacrificial death, but his showing the innermost meaning of the
Old Testament teachings. Thus, what follows in Matthew 5:18–42
reveals not a rejection of the law by Jesus but how he understands that
its teachings should be fulfilled. Other examples of this literary form
are found in Matthew 6:22–23; 10:34; Luke 10:16.

Chiasmic Parallelism

Another form of poetic parallelism involves a particular structure
called a chiasmas. In a chiasmas we have an inverting of parallel statements in the form of a b // B A. The first statement consists of two
parts (a and b); the second consists of two parts as well, but they are in
reverse order (B and A). This is best seen by way of some examples:

whoever *exalts* himself (a)

                will be *humbled* (b)
                and whoever *humbles* himself (B)

will be *exalted* (A) (Matt. 23:12).

No one can serve two masters
Either he will *hate* the one (a)

                and *love* the other (b)
                or he will be *devoted* to the one (B)

and *despise* the other (A)
You cannot serve both God and

For whoever wants to *save* his life (a)

                will *lose* it (b)
                but whoever *loses* his life for me
                and for the gospel (B)

will *save* it (A) (Mark 8:35).

It is apparent that the above are examples not only of chiasmic parallelism but of antithetical parallelism as well. Other examples of this parallelism can be found in Matthew 7:6 (dogs—a; pigs—b; trample [pigs
do this]—B; turn and tear you to pieces [dogs do this]—A); Mark 2:22
(wine—a; old wineskins—b; wine burst skins—B; wine lost—A [so

RSV]); 2:27 (Sabbath—a; man—b; man—B; Sabbath—A); 9:43 (hand—a; cut it off—b; maimed—B; two hands—a); 10:31 (first—a; last—b; last—B; first—A); Rom. 2:7 (a), 8(b), 9) (B), 10(A); Phil. 2:6(a), 7(b), 8(B), 9–11(A); Isa. 22:22 (opens—a; shuts—b; shuts—B; opens—A); 29:17 (Lebanon—a; fertile field—b; fertile field—B; forest—A); Jer. 2:19 (in Hebrew—will punish—a; your wickedness—b; your backsliding—B; will rebuke—A). It is evident once again that by knowing the literary form of this poetry, we are better able to understand how the various parts relate to one another and thus to understand what the biblical writers were seeking to convey when they expressed their meaning by using this literary form.

(Another poetic form that is sometimes mentioned is that of synthetic parallelism. This is the most ambiguous of the poetic forms, and there is confusion in defining it and understanding exactly how it functions. We shall not deal with it.)

Conclusion

The amount of poetry found in the Bible and in the teachings of Jesus is impressive. Clearly the world of the biblical writers was one in which people sought to express their thoughts using emotive and picturesque language. This is clearly seen in the poetry of the Bible, for the metaphorical nature of this material is impressive, and we cannot read it without "feeling" the heartbeat of the authors. It is clear that the writers felt deeply about what they were saying in this form of literature. They were not interested in merely conveying information, although their poetry certainly does this. They were seeking to elicit a decision and to impress their readers with the importance of what they were saying.

Another reason why poetry appears in such abundance in the Bible is because the poets' audiences were oral societies. How could a speaker assist hearers in retaining the divine message he was delivering? He could not expect his audience to take notes or to record his words on a cassette. As a result he placed his message in easy-to-remember forms. The rhythmic nature of poetry assists greatly in memory. An example can demonstrate this. If I were asked by someone to write out the first verse of the great hymn, "The Church's One Foundation," I would have no trouble with the first line. "The church's one foundation is Jesus Christ her Lord." After this, however, I would have trouble, but

I would begin to hum the tune and sing the hymn to myself. In this manner the remaining lines would become clear—"She is his new creation by water and the word . . . " Likewise, it is easier to remember the rhythmic content of Matthew 7:7–8 than a similar amount of material from Romans 3.

In our attempt to understand the meaning of this biblical material, we need to remember such things as the nature of poetry in contrast to prose (its use of picturesque and nonliteral language), and the particular form of the poetry (is it synonymous or antithetical parallelism, synonymous or step parallelism, etc.). To interpret poetry as if it were prose can only lead to misunderstanding. Whether we are interpreting prose or poetry, of course, we are still seeking to understand what the author meant when he wrote these words. However, the rules for the one literary form are different than the rules governing the other.

Questions

1. What is "poetic license"? Why is this necessary in poetry?
2. Read Proverbs 3–7. Do you find figurative language? Did you find more "synonymous" or "antithetical" parallelism?
3. Where else might we find poetry in the Bible?
4. What is the value of knowing if a passage is an example of synonymous or antithetical parallelism?

8

The Game of Jargon—Idioms

The most difficult form of literature to interpret is idioms. The reason is that in idioms the literal meaning of the words does not convey what an author meant by the use of these words. Frequently his meaning is quite different and even contrary to the normal use of these words. We can only know if a combination of words is an idiom by finding this same combination in different places and noting from the context that its meaning is different from the normal meaning conveyed by these words. We will then begin to see that these words belong together as a unit and must be interpreted as such.

I still remember upon my return from sabbatical study overseas when a friend said to me about something he had just purchased, "Bob, you ought to try it. It's really bad." I was totally confused by what he said. That same week I heard another person say "It's really bad" about something I knew he liked. Then I heard someone on television say the same thing, and she, too, was clearly using the expression in a positive sense. It began to dawn on me that during my time overseas the phrase "It is really bad" had become an idiom whose meaning was radically different from the literal meaning of those words. What people meant by this idiom was "It is really *good*."

Numerous examples of such idioms exist in the English language. We have all had people say to us, "Have a good day." Yet despite the fact that the wording of this expression is an imperative, we have never interpreted this as a command from our friends that we must have a good day. We have recognized that this is an idiom for "Good-bye." Similarly, the expression "God bless you" is not a command addressed to God demanding that he bless you. Rather, it is either a prayer such as "I pray that God may be gracious to you and bless you" or more likely "Gesundheit," something we say after a person sneezes even though we do not know why we say it. As for the greeting "How are you?" this is usually not to be thought of as a question regarding our health and well-being but simply "Hello." Idioms are good examples of the fact that the "meaning" of words is not determined by what the words mean in and of themselves but rather by what the author willed by those words.

The Love-Hate Imagery

In the Bible we encounter various idioms. In using these idioms the authors recognized that they were idioms and expected that their readers would interpret them as such. One of the most troubling of the biblical idioms is found in Malachi 1:2–3:

> "I have loved you," says the LORD. "But you ask, 'How have you loved us?' Was not Esau Jacob's brother?" the LORD says. "Yet I have loved Jacob, but Esau I have hated, and I have turned his mountains into a wasteland and left his inheritance to the desert jackals."

Paul in Romans 9:13, as he refers to God's election, quotes this passage and says, "Just as it is written: 'Jacob I loved, but Esau I hated.'" The troublesome nature of these verses is immediately apparent. How can a God who loves the world (John 3:16) hate Esau? If we look at the various commentaries on Romans, it is apparent that the idiomatic nature of these words is frequently missed.

In my own struggle with these passages and with Luke 14:26 ("If anyone comes to me and does not hate his father and mother, his wife and children, his brothers and sisters—yes, even his own life—he cannot be my disciple"), it was only when I came to understand the idiomatic nature of the love-hate contrast that these passages finally made sense. The key passage that helped me see this was Genesis 29:30–31: "So Jacob . . . *loved* Rachel *more* than Leah. . . . When the LORD saw that Leah was *hated* . . ." Note here that in the Revised Standard Version, which translates the Hebrew literally, the opposite of "loving more" is "hating"! To love someone (Rachel) more than another (Leah) is in the Hebrew idiom to love one (Rachel) and hate the other (Leah)! Other translations, rather than giving a word-for-word translation as the Revised Standard Version and King James Version do, seek to provide a thought-for-thought equivalent and translate the contrast "love more—not loved" (NIV), "loved—not loved" (NEB), and "love—unloved" (NRSV). The actual terminology used in the Hebrew text, however, is "love—hate." Yet surely the writer of Genesis knew that Jacob did not hate Leah. We know this because he describes their relationship as producing six sons and a daughter. Something other than "hate" must have been involved in their relationship. Jacob did love Leah, *but* he loved Rachel more.

The idiomatic nature of the love-hate contrast is also seen in Deuteronomy 21:15–17. None of the modern translations provides a word-for-word translation. However, the King James Version translates this passage as follows:

> If a man have two wives, one beloved, and another hated, and they have born him children, both the beloved and the hated; and if the firstborn son be hers that was hated: Then it shall be, when he maketh his sons to inherit that which he hath, that he may not make the son of the beloved firstborn before the son of the hated, which is indeed the firstborn: But he shall acknowledge the son of the hated for the firstborn, by giving him a double portion of all that he hath; for he is the beginning of his strength; the right of the firstborn is his.

The modern translations, recognizing the idiomatic nature of this contrast, translate the passage using such contrasts as "loves one but not the other" (NIV); "one loved and the other disliked" (RSV; NRSV); "one loved and the other unloved" (NEB; REB). Again, the issue is not that one wife is loved and the other is hated-unloved-disliked. The idiom speaks rather of one wife being loved "more" than the other. This does not mean that the less-loved wife is hated and loathed. It means rather that she, like Leah, is loved less. However, the way that this was expressed in the Hebrew of that day was by the idiom of one wife being loved and the other hated.

The same idiom also appears in Proverbs 13:24, "He who spares the rod hates his son, but he who loves him is careful to discipline him," and in Luke 14:26. In the latter passage to "hate" father and mother means to love Jesus more. This is evident from the parallel in Matthew 10:37, "Anyone who loves his father or mother more than me is not worthy of me; anyone who loves his son or daughter more than me is not worthy of me." Whereas Luke provides a "word-for-word" translation of Jesus' actual words, Matthew has given us a "thought-for-thought" one. What Jesus demands of his followers is not dislike or hate toward their parents. On the contrary, those who place Jesus before everything else will love their parents, wives, and children even more than before. However, the followers of Jesus must always place their love and commitment to Jesus before their love for family. Jesus demands not lesser love for family but greater love for him, and love for family will increase continually even as our love for him increases.

Other Biblical Idioms

Another idiom that has caused great difficulty is found in Psalm 137:8–9: "O Daughter of Babylon, doomed to destruction, happy is he who repays you for what you have done to us—he who seizes your infants and dashes them against the rocks" (cf. also Ps. 109:6–15). The repulsive nature of the imagery is evident to all. How could the psalmist wish this upon the children of Babylon, even if they were his enemies? Yet the idiomatic nature of the saying means something different than a desire for bloodthirsty vengeance. The imagery found here was tragically enough not uncommon in warfare (2 Kings 8:12; Isa. 13:16, 18; Hos. 10:14; 13:16; Nah. 3:10). What the psalmist is describing, however, is not a wish for vicious revenge upon Babylon but a desire for God's justice to be accomplished. He wishes for God's righteous judgment to fall upon the evil kingdom of Babylon. In his desire for divine justice he uses the imagery of his day to describe the overthrow of nations. It is interesting to note that in several ancient illustrations of a king's reign we find that the son of the king is sitting on his father's lap and the defeated and subject peoples are depicted beneath not the father's feet but the son's! Thus, the judgment of the king of Babylon must also involve the judgment of his sons. Only in this way will the evil dynasty be judged and destroyed. This idiom therefore should be understood and interpreted in light of the imagery of its day and what the author is seeking to describe by the use of this imagery. The author is longing for the divine justice to manifest itself in the overthrow of this evil empire.

Other idioms found within the Bible involve: "our hearts melted" (Josh. 2:11; 5:1; 7:5; 2 Sam. 17:10; Isa. 13:7; 19:1; Nah. 2:10) for the loss of courage; the stars, sun, and moon not giving light (Isa. 13:9–11; 24:23; Ezek. 32:7–8; Joel 2:10, 31; 3:15; Amos 8:9; Hab. 3:11; Acts 2:14–21) for divine intervention in history, whether for blessing or judgment; becoming "as numerous as the stars in the sky and as the sand of the seashore" (Gen. 22:17; 26:4; 32:12; Exod. 32:13; Deut. 10:22; 28:62; Josh. 11:4; Judg. 7:12; 1 Chron. 27:23; Nah. 3:16; Heb. 11:12) for a large number; "weeping and gnashing of teeth" (Lam. 2:16; Matt. 8:12; 13:42, 50; 22:13; 24:51; 25:30; Luke 13:28) for experiencing severe sorrow and loss; "not a man was left" (Josh. 8:17; Judg. 4:16; 2 Kings 10:21; cf. also Num. 21:35; Deut. 3:3) for winning a great victory.

Questions

1. Can you think of a present-day idiom whose meaning is quite different from the literal meaning of the words?

2. How do idioms demonstrate that meaning is not a property of the text?

3. How do idioms demonstrate that the etymology of words is of little value in understanding the "meaning" of the text?

9

The Game
of Exaggeration—Hyperbole

A s has been noted on several occasions, the Bible contains a great deal of hyperbolic language. Proverbs, poetry, and prophecy by their very nature use exaggerated language (see pp. 83–115), as do most forms of commissive language (see pp. 73–74). Some Christians find it difficult to believe that there is "exaggeration" in the Bible. They associate exaggeration with inexactness and imprecision. Worse yet, in the minds of some, exaggeration is a synonym for falsehood.

The use of hyperbole or exaggeration, however, is a perfectly acceptable literary form when shared by writer and reader. When used in this way, it is a powerful form that enables the writer to convey not just factual information but also feelings and emotions. In fact, it is very difficult to communicate certain things apart from exaggeration. How do two people in love express their love to one another? It is certainly not in the precise language of science! On the contrary, they may use poetry that is filled with metaphor and hyperbole. Or they may use prose, but this, too, will be filled with hyperbole. The one form they will certainly not use is the literal precision of a chemistry lab report. In the communication of lovers, whether between a man and a woman or between the psalmist and his God, hyperbole is necessary.

What makes hyperbole or exaggeration illegitimate is when the writer is not sharing with his reader that he is using this form of language. Unless shared, this form of language is deceitful and dishonest. When a

123

Love Letter

October 1, 1993

My Dearest Joan,

_____

_____ heart
aches_____

_____ die unless
I see you soon.

_____

_____

_____
can't live without you_____

_____ hold my
breath until see you _____

_____

_____

_____

Chemistry Lab **Report**

Student's Name   Date
P.O.#   Instructor

Column Chromatography

_____

_____

Reaction
Fluorine $\underset{CH_3COOH}{\overset{Na_2\,Cr_3\,O_7}{\rule{2cm}{0.4pt}}}$ Fluorenene

_____

_____

Procedure
  Dissolve some Fluorine in 25
ml. acetic acid _____
heat at 80° for 15 minutes in a
water bath_____

_____

Observations

_____

_____

man tells his beloved that he is "sick and would die if he never saw her again," this conveys the truth that he deeply loves and misses her, even if he feels perfectly well at the time. On the other hand, for an employee to phone in and state that he or she cannot come to work because of being ill, while feeling perfectly well at the time, is to lie. The acceptability of this literary form of communication depends on its being shared. When shared, it is a very powerful and effective form of communication. When not shared, it is either a bad example of miscommunication, of the writer's incompetence and inability to express what he or she meant, or it is a deliberate attempt to deceive and mislead.

Exaggeration can be subdivided into two types: overstatement in which what is said is exaggerated but literally possible, and hyperbole in which what is said is so exaggerated that it is literally impossible. We shall not concern ourselves in this chapter with this distinction. The issue is not so much "if" there is exaggeration in the Bible but how to detect it. Its presence in the Bible is clear from the following examples:

You blind guides! You strain out a gnat but swallow a camel. (Matt. 23:24)

Why do you look at the speck of sawdust in your brother's eye and pay no attention to the plank in your own eye? How can you say to your brother, "Let me take the speck out of your eye," when all the time there is a plank in your own eye? You hypocrite, first take the plank out of your own eye, and then you will see clearly to remove the speck from your brother's eye. (Matt. 7:3–4)

Children, how hard it is to enter the kingdom of God! It is easier for a camel to go through the eye of a needle than for a rich man to enter the kingdom of God. (Mark 10:24b–25)

I am poured out like water, and all my bones are out of joint. My heart has turned to wax; it has melted away within me. (Ps. 22:14; cf. Lam. 2:11)

And all the people went up after him [King Solomon], playing flutes and rejoicing greatly, so that the ground shook with the sound. (1 Kings 1:40)

Clearly none of the above was meant to be taken literally. In the first example, which is also a pun in Aramaic (Jesus' mother tongue), it is obvious that a person cannot swallow a camel. Similarly, a plank cannot fit in someone's eye. And despite all the unsuccessful attempts to find a gate called "the eye of a needle," the saying about "a camel going through the eye of a needle" was intended by Jesus to be interpreted as an example of hyperbole. The psalmist also did not intend for his readers to think that his "heart" had changed from a solid to a liquid, and the writer of 1 Kings did not want his readers to believe that an actual earthquake took place. These are all examples of hyperbole.

Most people are intuitively able to determine if a passage contains hyperbole. They just "know" that such passages should not be interpreted literally. Yet in the history of the church there have been numerous examples where individuals have not recognized the presence of this literary form, and this has led to drastic results. During the 1970s within the "Jesus movement" several groups argued that their members were to "hate" their parents on the basis of Luke 14:26. In supposed obedience to the biblical teaching (and in ignorance of the hyperbole present in this verse and of the clear teachings of the Bible elsewhere) young people actually believed they should hate their parents. At other times some have mutilated themselves due to the misinterpretation of Matthew 5:29–30. (In the context of lust these verses speak about gouging out one's eye and cutting off one's hand in order to avoid the damnation of hell.)

There are a number of helpful rules that enable us to recognize if a statement in the Bible contains exaggeration.

1. The statement is literally impossible. The passages listed above are all examples of this. They are simply impossible. The realities of life do not permit them to be true in a literal sense. Compare also:

> I will surely bless you and make your descendants as numerous as the stars in the sky and as the sand on the seashore. (Gen. 22:17)

> Saul and Jonathan—in life they were loved and gracious, and in death they were not parted. They were swifter than eagles, they were stronger than lions. (2 Sam. 1:23)

In such cases, the authors expected their readers to recognize the non-literal quality of these statements and to interpret them as expressive examples of certain truths (God would bless Abraham and his descendants; Saul and Jonathan were mighty warriors). Those truths were, however, conveyed by the use of hyperbole.

2. The statement conflicts with what the speaker says elsewhere. This can be shown most easily in the case of Jesus. Note the following examples:

> If anyone comes to me and does not hate his father and mother, his wife and children, his brothers and sisters—yes, even his own life—he cannot be my disciple. (Luke 14:26)

> But when you pray, go into your room, close the door and pray to your Father, who is unseen. Then your Father, who sees what is done in secret, will reward you. (Matt. 6:6)

It is clear that Jesus' statement about hating parents conflicts with his teachings in Mark 7:9–13; 10:19, which speak of honoring parents. It also conflicts with his teaching concerning loving enemies (Luke 6:27), for if we were to hate our parents, this would make them enemies and thus qualify them to be recipients of our love! Similarly, his statement to pray privately in your room conflicts with the very prayer he taught his disciples, which is corporate in nature (*"Our* Father . . . Give *us* . . . *our* daily bread" [Matt. 6:9–13]).

Other examples of this can be found in Isaiah 11:6–9 and 35:8–10, both of which cannot be literally true, for in the first instance lions are present in the kingdom of God and in the second they are excluded.

3. The statement conflicts with the actions of the speaker elsewhere. It is true that religious teachers can contradict their teachings by their conduct. Jesus referred to this when he said, "The teachers of the law and the Pharisees sit in Moses' seat. So you must obey them and do everything they tell you. But do not do what they do, for they do not practice what they preach" (Matt. 23:2–3). Good teachers, however, seek to demonstrate what they mean by their teachings through their actions. Thus, if Jesus makes a statement that conflicts with his actions, this may be an indication that his statement contains hyperbole. Some examples of this are:

> Again, you have heard that it was said to the people long ago, "Do not break your oath, but keep the oaths you have made to the Lord." But I tell you, Do not swear at all: either by heaven, for it is God's throne; or by the earth, for it is his footstool; or by Jerusalem, for it is the city of the Great King. And do not swear by your head, for you cannot make even one hair white or black. Simply let your "Yes" be "Yes" and your "No," "No"; anything beyond this comes from the evil one. (Matt. 5:33–37)

> Do not suppose that I have come to bring peace to the earth. I did not come to bring peace, but a sword. (Matt. 10:34)

In the midst of the debate among his contemporaries as to what oaths should be kept, Jesus states that people should not swear at all. Although some Christians interpret this literally and refuse to swear even in a court of law, it is evident that Jesus was using hyperbole in this statement. One reason is that Jesus in practice accepted the legitimacy of such oaths. This is seen in the account of his trial. During his trial Jesus remained silent until he was placed by the high priest under an oath, "I charge you under oath by the living God: Tell us if you are the Christ, the Son of God" (Matt. 26:63b). According to Leviticus 5:1 (cf. also 1 Kings 22:16; Prov. 29:24) when placed under this oath, a person was obligated to respond. To remain silent was to admit guilt. Jesus reveals that he accepted the legitimacy of this oath, because at this point he broke his silence (Matt. 26:64).

With respect to the saying in Matthew 10:34 it is obvious from Jesus' nonresistance at Gethsemene (Mark 14:43–50) and his forgiveness of his enemies (Luke 23:34) that this saying is an example of hyperbole. (Such sayings of Jesus as found in Matt. 5:9; 10:12–13; Mark 5:34; and

Luke 19:42 also reveal that this saying should not be interpreted literally. [See rule 2 above.]) Likewise Jesus' saying about praying in private (Matt. 6:6) and hating parents (Luke 14:26) conflict with his behavior in Mark 6:46; 14:32; Luke 6:12; 9:28; Matthew 19:13 and John 19:26–27; Luke 2:51 respectively.

4. The statement conflicts with the teachings of the Old Testament. Jesus' understanding of the Old Testament can be seen from two of his statements. In the first Jesus says,

> Do not think that I have come to abolish the Law or the Prophets; I have not come to abolish them but to fulfill them. . . . Anyone who breaks one of the least of these commandments and teaches others to do the same will be called least in the kingdom of heaven, but whoever practices and teaches these commands will be called great in the kingdom of heaven. (Matt. 5:17–19)

The second is found in Jesus' summary of the greatest commandment, where he responds to the question, "Of all the commandments, which is the most important?"

> The most important one . . . is this: 'Hear, O Israel, the Lord our God, the Lord is one. Love the Lord your God with all your heart and with all your soul and with all your mind and with all your strength.' The second is this: 'Love your neighbor as yourself.' There is no commandment greater than these. (Mark 12:29–31)

It is clear that Jesus saw his teachings as being in harmony with and in fulfillment of the ethical teachings of the Old Testament. (Cf. also Mark 10:17–19.) If there are exceptions (Mark 10:1–12), these are rare and simply prove the rule.

If we therefore find a saying of Jesus that clearly and radically conflicts with the Old Testament, this suggests that Jesus may be using hyperbole. Thus, Jesus' saying about hating parents (Luke 14:26), which clearly violates the teachings of the Old Testament and the Ten Commandments (Exod. 20:12; cf. also Lev. 19:18; Deut. 6:5), is an example of hyperbole, as is his prohibition against swearing an oath (Matt. 5:33–37; cf. Lev. 5:1; 19:12 [cf. Exod. 20:7]; Num. 30:2–15; Deut. 23:21–23 and those instances where God himself swore such an oath—Deut. 1:8; Pss. 110:4; 132:11; Isa. 14:24; etc.).

5. The statement conflicts with the teachings of the New Testament. In rule 4 we pointed out that Jesus' ethical thinking was based on that found in the Old Testament. Thus, we can expect them to be alike. This will help us understand Jesus' meaning. The thinking of the New Testament writers was also similar to that of Jesus. They will therefore likewise provide assistance in our attempt to understand the meaning of Jesus' teachings. As a result, if we find a statement of Jesus that tends to conflict with that of the New Testament writers, this should give us pause and cause us to question whether we have an example of hyperbole in the statement. It would be strange indeed if Jesus' contemporaries and followers would have radically misunderstood or misinterpreted the teachings of their Lord. For the evangelical Christian this possibility is even more unlikely, since the writers of the New Testament are understood as the divinely inspired interpreters of Jesus' teachings. Thus, if we find a saying of Jesus, which appears to conflict with the teachings of the New Testament, this may be a clue that Jesus was using hyperbole.

An example of this is Jesus' teaching about not swearing an oath. This stands in sharp conflict with the practice of Paul (Rom. 1:9; 2 Cor. 1:23; Gal. 1:20; Phil. 1:8) who swears such oaths and with the fact that God swore an oath (Acts 2:30; Heb. 6:16–17; 7:20–22). Other examples include Jesus' command to hate parents (Luke 14:26; cf. Eph. 6:1–3; Col. 3:20; 1 John 3:10–11; 4:7; etc.) and the following:

Give to the one who asks you, and do not turn away from the one who wants to borrow from you. (Matt. 5:42)

Judge not, that you be not judged. (Matt. 7:1 RSV)

It is clear that Paul knew of instances where one should not give to the one asking, for he reminds the Thessalonians, "For even when we were with you, we gave you this rule: 'If a man will not work, he shall not eat'" (2 Thess. 3:10). As to the prohibition on judging, similar teaching is found in Romans 14:10 and 1 Corinthians 4:5, but Paul judges in 1 Corinthians 5:3 and rebukes the church in 1 Corinthians 6:1–6 for not judging in a particular instance. And how can someone rebuke (1 Tim. 5:20; 2 Tim. 4:2) without judging? The New Testament therefore understands Jesus' teachings as prohibiting the negative and critical judgment of others. Yet in the context of love and the purity of the church, judgment is called for at times.

6. The statement is interpreted by another biblical writer in a non-literal way. There are a number of instances when a biblical author interprets a saying found elsewhere in a manner that indicates that he understood the original sayings as being hyperbolic. This can be seen quite clearly when we compare the Matthean and Lukan versions of Jesus' statement about hating parents:

> If anyone comes to me and does not hate his father and mother, his wife and children, his brothers and sisters—yes, even his own life—he cannot be my disciple. (Luke 14:26)

> Anyone who loves his father or mother more than me is not worthy of me; anyone who loves his son or daughter more than me is not worthy of me. (Matt. 10:37)

What we have in these two statements are two versions of the same saying of Jesus. Most scholars agree that the Lukan version is more authentic, more like the original saying of Jesus. (The reason for this is the difficulty of the saying in Luke. It is easier to understand Matthew explaining Jesus' harder original saying [the Lukan version] than to understand Luke making more difficult Jesus' easier original saying [the Matthew version].) What we have in these two accounts are variant philosophies of translations by the Evangelists. Luke was led to provide his readers with a literal translation of Jesus' saying. He did so by using a "word-for-word" translation. Matthew, however, was led to give a "thought-for-thought" translation of Jesus' teaching. Both sayings, properly understood, convey the same meaning of Jesus. One (Luke) does so by retaining the original hyperbole in the saying; the other (Matthew) does so by eliminating the hyperbole and interpreting for his readers what Jesus meant by his hyperbole.

Another example of this is found in Jesus' teaching on divorce. We possess three distinct instances of this in the New Testament:

> Anyone who divorces his wife and marries another woman commits adultery against her. (Mark 10:11)

> Anyone who divorces his wife and marries another woman commits adultery, and the man who marries a divorced woman commits adultery. (Luke 16:18)

> To the married I give this command (not I, but the Lord [i.e., this command which I am giving was given by Jesus]): A wife must not separate

from her husband. But if she does, she must remain unmarried or else be reconciled to her husband. And a husband must not divorce his wife. (1 Cor. 7:10–11)

In the Matthean version of this teaching we have the following:

I tell you that anyone who divorces his wife, except for marital unfaithfulness, and marries another woman commits adultery. (19:9)

But I tell you that anyone who divorces his wife, except for marital unfaithfulness, causes her to become an adulteress, and anyone who marries the divorced woman commits adultery. (5:32)

In my understanding what Matthew has done by his famous "exception clause" is to reveal that he understood Jesus' teaching to be hyperbolic in nature. In the Pharisaic discussion of what were the legitimate reasons for divorcing a wife (Mark 10:2) Jesus replies that all divorce is wrong. There is no such thing as a "good" divorce. Divorce always reveals a failure of the divine purpose. To enter into a discussion of the legitimate reasons for divorce would misdirect the focus of his hearers from God's hatred of divorce (Mal. 2:16) to discussion of those instances when divorce may be the lesser of two evils. In the context of Jesus the former was by far the more important. In the context of Matthew, however, the Evangelist as an inspired interpreter of Jesus' words indicates that there is an instance when divorce is permissible, although not demanded. Paul in 1 Corinthians 7:12–15 may give another.

The following is another example of where a biblical writer indicates that a saying of Jesus' found elsewhere is hyperbolic:

Do not suppose that I have come to bring peace to the earth. I did not come to bring peace, but a sword. (Matt. 10:34)

Do you think I came to bring peace on earth? No, I tell you, but division. (Luke 12:51)

Here Luke has eliminated the hyperbolic metaphor, which could be misinterpreted as political in nature, and translated the word "sword" according to its meaning. What Jesus meant was not that he had come to bring political insurrection, the sword of rebellion, but that he came to be God's divider, the divine watershed, who would divide all humanity into one of two parts: believers/unbelievers; Christians/non-Christians; sheep/goats; saved/unsaved.

We can also note how Matthew interpreted Jesus' saying about not judging in Matthew 7:1 by such statements as 7:6 (How do we know whom not to throw our pearls before without some sort of judging?) and 18:15–17 (How do we perform church discipline without judging?).

7. The statement has not been literally fulfilled. At times we encounter a saying of Jesus that has not been fulfilled in a literal sense. Examples of this are the following:

> As he was leaving the temple, one of his disciples said to him, "Look, Teacher! What massive stones! What magnificent buildings!" "Do you see all these great buildings?" replied Jesus. "Not one stone here will be left on another; every one will be thrown down." (Mark 13:1–2)

> Ask and it will be given to you; seek and you will find; knock and the door will be opened to you. For everyone who asks receives; he who seeks finds; and to him who knocks, the door will be opened. (Matt. 7:7–8)

> "Have faith in God," Jesus answered. "I tell you the truth, if anyone says to this mountain, 'Go, throw yourself into the sea,' and does not doubt in his heart but believes that what he says will happen, it will be done for him. Therefore I tell you, whatever you ask for in prayer, believe that you have received it, and it will be yours." (Mark 11:22–24)

It is evident that despite the horrendous destruction of Jerusalem in A.D. 70 there still exist stones that are standing on one another. Thus, if we interpret Jesus' saying literally this saying has not been fulfilled. Yet when we reflect on the terrible destruction that the city experienced, the use of hyperbole by Jesus to describe this is perfectly understandable. Only hyperbolic language can do justice to the tremendous destruction that Jerusalem experienced at that time.

As for the sayings on prayer, in my life I know of prayers that have not been answered. Most Christians will admit the same. James, in fact, says this when he writes, "When you ask, you do not receive, because you ask with wrong motives, that you may spend what you get on your pleasures" (4:3). James states that one of the prerequisites for God answering prayer is that the motives must be correct. In Mark 11:22–24 another prerequisite is listed: praying in faith. Needless to say, Jesus did not intend his hearers to interpret his saying in Matthew 7:7–8 as a guarantee that any prayer would be answered, regardless of how absurd and dishonoring to God it might be. Jesus assumed that all such asking/seeking/knocking would be done according to the will of God, with right motives. He assumed that his followers would always pray, whether they expressly stated it or not, "Yet not what I will, but what you will" (Mark 14:36). However, to include in Matthew 7:7–8 such presuppositions or requirements would have detracted from what Jesus was seeking to teach. In this saying Jesus wanted to assure his followers that their Father in heaven was eager to hear and answer their prayers. To list in the saying various conditions or assumptions would have detracted from the point he was trying to make and shift the focus of attention from God's desire to answer prayer to the preconditions for prayer. Jesus did not want to do this, and thus used hyperbole to reveal his point.

Another example of this rule can be found in the saying of Jesus in Matthew 26:52, "all who draw the sword will die by the sword." All mercenaries and warriors do not die young. Some profit quite nicely from war. Nevertheless, if this saying had been read in a church in Berlin or Tokyo after World War II, would any in the audience have found fault with its hyperbolic nature?

8. The statement would not achieve its desired goal. It is apparent that if some sayings were carried out literally, they would not achieve what the speaker intended. Removing an eye (Matt. 5:29–30) would not solve the problem of lust (note Matt. 5:28). People can still lust with the left eye or without any eyes! It is what comes out of the heart that defiles a person (Mark 7:20–23). Surely Jesus knew that such self-mutilation would not bring about the goal he sought. As a result, this must be an example of hyperbole by which Jesus sought to demonstrate the importance and necessity of repenting in order to enter the kingdom of God.

9. The statement uses a literary form prone to exaggeration. We have already pointed out that there are certain literary forms, such as proverbs, prophecy, poetry, and idioms, which are prone to exaggeration. Without reduplicating what has already been said concerning these forms (see pp. 83–115), note the examples of hyperbole in the following:

- Proverbs—Proverbs 3:9–10; 10:3–4; 13:21; 15:1; Matthew 6:21; 10:24; 26:52; Mark 6:4; Luke 16:10; etc.
- Prophecy—Isaiah 13:9–11 (describing the destruction of Babylon); Jeremiah 4:11–13, 23–26; Mark 13:2, 13a, 14–16, 24–25.

- Poetry—Judges 5 (compare with Judg. 4); Exodus 15:1–21 (compare with Exod. 14:21–29); Matthew 5:39–41; 6:5–6, 24; 7:7–8; 10:34; etc.
- Idioms—Deuteronomy 21:15–17; Joshua 2:11; 5:1; 7:5; Malachi 1:2–3; Matthew 8:12; 13:42, 50; 22:13; 24:51; 25:30; etc.

10. The statement uses universal language. Although the terms "all," "everyone," "no one," and the like can be used in a literal sense (Luke 13:3, 5; Rom. 3:10, 23; 2 Cor. 5:10), there are times when the unqualified use of such terms suggest the possibility that what is being said may be hyperbolic in nature. Some examples of this can be found in the following:

> From the least to the greatest, all are greedy for gain; prophets and priests alike, all practice deceit. (Jer. 6:13)

> "'If you can'?" said Jesus. "Everything is possible for him who believes." (Mark 9:23)

> Give to everyone who asks you, and if anyone takes what belongs to you, do not demand it back. (Luke 6:30)

It is evident that in the first instance "all" is hyperbolic in nature, for Jeremiah was himself a prophet and he was not guilty of the charge. Similarly, it is evident that not "everything" is possible for the Christian. The believer cannot become God! He cannot cause God to cease to exist! And what Christian parent would tolerate giving his children everything they asked for? Love would deny things that would harm them!

The use of universal language should warn us of the possibility that what is being said is being said hyperbolically. For other examples, see Matthew 10:32 (cf. 7:21–22); 23:3, 35; Mark 2:21–22; 10:11–12; 13:30; Luke 5:39.

Conclusion

The use of hyperbole in the Bible is evident. The degree to which it is used is not always acknowledged, but it is more extensive than most people realize. The recognition of hyperbole in the biblical text, however, is not the end of the process of interpretation. It is actually only the beginning. We must try to understand the meaning this language seeks to convey. At times the meaning of the saying is self-evident, once we recognize that it contains exaggeration (Matt. 6:6; 10:34; Mark 10:25). At times we are assisted by the immediate context in which the saying is found (cf. Matt. 7:3–4 with 7:1; Matt. 10:34 with 10:35–37) or by the larger context of the author's (Jesus') teaching (cf. Luke 14:26 with Matt. 10:38–39) or the biblical teaching in general (cf. Luke 14:26 with Exod. 20:12; Matt. 5:42 with 2 Thess. 3:10).

Once we have understood the meaning of the hyperbolic statement, we must also ask why this meaning was framed in this particular literary form. At times this form may have been used as a mnemonic device, to help the hearers/readers remember the saying. It is clear that Jesus' statement about hating parents (Luke 14:26) is not easily forgotten! Yet the presence of hyperbole also reveals the importance of what is being said for the author. We tend to use hyperbole to emphasize what is important. We do not exaggerate trivial truths. Rather, we use hyperbole when we seek to convey something that we think is important. As a result, we need to pay special attention when we find this literary form in the Bible. When we come across such a statement, we need to remind ourselves that this was so important that the author used exaggeration to reveal what he meant. Thus, the meaning of such a statement should be especially significant to the reader.

Questions

1. Can you recall when you recently used exaggeration in speaking or writing to someone? How did you let your audience know that you were exaggerating? Why did you use exaggeration?

2. In which of the following situations would you tend to expect exaggeration: a grandparent describing his or her grandchildren; a person in an accident reporting what happened to a policeman; describing an illness to a doctor; telling of the fish you caught on vacation; testifying in a court; hearing a poet read his or her poetry; a description of the addition to the house that you want a carpenter to build; etc.

3. How is the issue of "truth" related to the use of exaggeration?

4. Is Matthew 17:10 hyperbolic? Luke 10:19?

10

The Game
of Comparison—Parables

Perhaps the best known and most famous literary form found in the Bible is the parable. This is especially true of such parables of Jesus as the good Samaritan, the prodigal son, the wise and foolish maidens, and the four soils. Defining exactly what a parable is in the Old Testament (*mashal*) or New Testament (*parabolē*), however, is difficult. These terms can refer to a proverb (1 Sam 24:13; Ezek. 18:2–3; Luke 4:23; 6:39); satire or taunt (Pss. 44:11; 69:11; Isa. 14:3–4; Hab. 2:4); riddle (Pss. 49:4; 78:2; Prov. 1:6); figurative saying (Mark 7:14–17; Luke 5:36–38); extended simile or similitude (Matt. 13:33; Mark 4:30–32; Luke 15:8–10); story parable (Matt. 25:1–13; Luke 14:16–24; 15:11–32; 16:1–8); example parable (Matt. 18:23–25; Luke 10:29–37; 12:16–21; 16:19–31); and even an allegory (Judg. 9:7–20; Ezek. 16:1–5; 17:2–10; 20:49–21:5; Mark 4:3–9, 13–20; 12:1–11). The two biblical terms carry a broad range of meanings, but basic to each is the idea of a comparison between two different things. Something is likened to something it is not.

The real, life-like quality of the parables, especially the parables of Jesus, has frequently caused interpreters to forget that the parable is a fictional literary form. This literary form consists of two parts: a picture part, or the story proper, and a reality part, or the comparison to which it is likened. The picture itself does not describe an actual historical event. It is a fictional creation that came into being out of the mind of its author. Thus, we should not confuse it with biblical narrative, for in a biblical narrative the picture describes a historical event that really happened. Thus, in a biblical narrative it is perfectly legitimate to ask such questions as, Why did Joseph tell his brothers about his dream (Gen. 37:5–11)? Exactly what was it that defeated the armies of Sennacherib, king of Assyria, as they lay siege to Jerusalem (2 Kings 19:35–37)? Why did Paul and Barnabas disagree about taking John Mark on a second missionary journey (Acts 15:36–41)? What happened to Paul when he was tried in Rome (Acts 28)? It may not be possible to answer such questions, but they are legitimate because they are being asked with respect to historical narrative.

On the other hand, we cannot raise such questions with respect to parables. We cannot ask: Why in the parable of the prodigal son was the older brother out in the field when the prodigal returned (Luke 15:25)? There is no historical answer to this question. The two brothers never had historical existence. They are simply literary creations of Jesus. The older brother was out in the field because Jesus wanted him out in the field, and this is Jesus' story. Similarly, we cannot ask: How was it that the father saw his younger son while he was still at a distance (Luke 15:20)? Was it by chance or was he continually searching for him? Did he have good eyes? Nor can we ask: How did the older brother respond to his father's appeal (Luke 15:31–32)? Did he eventually repent of his attitude and accept his younger brother? And we cannot ask: Who took care of the ninety-nine sheep while the man searched for the one that was lost (Luke 15:4)? Such questions confuse the genre of parable with that of historical narrative. The father saw his younger son while he was still at a distance because Jesus wanted him to! The older brother could not respond to his father's appeal because he never existed in real life. He is only a fictional character and his fictional existence ceased when the parable ended. As to who would take care of the ninety-nine sheep, Jesus, the story-teller, would take care of them.

We must not confuse a life-like parable, which is a fictional creation, with a biblical narrative referring to a historical event. Of course, the reality to which the picture part of a parable refers is real and historical. In other words, the "meaning" Jesus intended and its various implications continue, but we must not address the picture part of a parable, which is fictional, with questions that are appropriate only to non-fictional literary forms such as biblical narrative.

Because of the fictional nature of parables, it is not surprising that at times we find unreal elements in them. We thus find unusual exaggeration as in the parable of the unforgiving servant who was forgiven ten thousand talents (Matt. 18:24). Herod's entire annual income was only nine hundred talents! We also find at times unusual circumstances: all ten maidens fall asleep (Matt. 25:5); all the invited guests, after accepting the first invitation, decline the final invitation to come to the banquet (Luke 14:18). Yet except for one or two Old Testament parables (Judg. 9:7–20; Ezek. 17:2–10), the parables of the Bible, especially the parables of Jesus, portray the everyday experiences of the real world.

Basic Principles for Interpreting Parables

Throughout the history of the church the parables have been interpreted allegorically. According to this method, the details in the picture part of a parable all have a corresponding point of comparison in the reality part. Perhaps the most famous example of this is Augustine's interpretation of the parable of the good Samaritan. According to Augustine the picture parts and the reality parts of the parable correspond as follows:

The man going down to Jericho	=	Adam
Jerusalem from which he was going	=	City of Heavenly Peace
Jericho	=	The moon, which signifies our morality (there is a play here on the terms "moon" and "Jericho" in Hebrew)
Robbers	=	Devil and his angels
Stripping him	=	Taking away his immortality
Beating him	=	Persuading him to sin
Leaving him half-dead	=	Due to sin, he was dead spiritually, but half-alive, due to his knowledge of God
Priest	=	Priesthood of the Old Testament, i.e., the Law
Levite	=	Ministry of the Old Testament, i.e., the Prophets
Good Samaritan	=	Christ

Binding of the wounds	=	Restraint placed upon sin
Oil	=	Comfort of good hope
Wine	=	Exhortation to spirited work
Beast	=	Body of Christ
Inn	=	Church
Two denarii	=	Two commandments of love
Innkeeper	=	Apostle Paul
Return of the Good Samaritan	=	Resurrection of Christ

A Parable Teaches a Basic Point

It has already been pointed out that the term "parable" covers a broad range of meanings in the Bible. Basic to all, however, is a comparison of two dissimilar things. In an extended comparison, such as the parable of the good Samaritan, should we look for a string of various comparisons or a single, basic comparison? In other words, should we seek to interpret a biblical parable as an allegory, somewhat along the lines of Augustine and the other early church fathers, or should we seek to interpret it as an extended picture that seeks to establish a single, basic point of comparison?

In the parable of the good Samaritan, is it important that the man was going down from Jerusalem to Jericho? It does not appear so. The parable would not change if the man had been going "up" from Jericho to Jerusalem. Would the meaning of the parable change if the innkeeper had been given three denarii rather than two? No doubt if he had, the allegorical method of interpretation would have seen in this a clear reference to the Trinity, but the meaning of the parable would not have changed. These details were added to the parable in order to provide local color and interest, but they do not carry with them a corresponding reality. These additional details do not make a parable into an allegory. Similarly in the parable of the prodigal son, such details as the returning son being given a robe, sandals, a signet ring, and a fatted calf for a feast do not possess a corresponding reality. It is true that the early church saw in them the return of the original righteousness that Adam lost (the robe), Christian baptism (the ring), and the Lord's Supper (the fatted calf and the feast), but the Pharisees and teachers of the law in Jesus' audience would never have interpreted the parable in this manner, and the parable was addressed to them (Luke 15:3). These picture parts demonstrate the great love of the father and his full acceptance of his son. Thus, they help illustrate an aspect of the point of the parable (God's love for the outcasts), but they do not possess any specific meaning in themselves.

This understanding receives support from the way metaphors and comparisons function. If someone were to ask the question, "What is God like?" I might reply, "God is like a loving Father who . . . " In so doing I would have a basic point of comparison in mind. If someone, however, then asked, "Well then who is God's wife?" this would illegitimately press the point of comparison further than was intended. There was only one basic reality I was seeking to illustrate by this metaphor. Ultimately any comparison will break down when pressed. The only comparison that will not break down is something like "God is like God." But this is no longer a comparison and serves no purpose. Every comparison of two unlike things must sooner or later break down. The fact is that the purpose of an analogy is to convey a basic point of comparison between the picture and the reality to which it corresponds.

If we keep this in mind, we will be less troubled by those parables in which characters exhibit questionable, if not immoral, behavior. For instance, in the parable of the unjust steward the behavior of the steward is clearly immoral. (He is only called "dishonest" after the activities described in Luke 16:4–7.) The commendation of the unjust steward, however, is due to his "shrewdness," not to his dishonesty. The point of the parable involves acting decisively in preparing for the coming judgment. (In the setting of Jesus this may have referred to the crisis caused by the coming of the kingdom of God.) If we do not press the details of the parable but are content with its one basic point of comparison, the parable does not cause confusion. Even shrewd thieves can illustrate a basic point. Similarly, in the parable of the wise and foolish maidens (Matt. 25:1–13) the fact that the wise maidens were "selfish" (v. 9) should not be pressed. The main point of the parable is clear enough: "Be prepared as the wise maidens were." Needless to say, Jesus assumed that his hearers would know from his other teachings how to be prepared; Matthew also assumed that his readers would know this from having read Matthew 1:1–24:51. The same is true with respect to the deceitful character of the man who discovered treasure hidden in a field (Matt. 13:44). In this parable Jesus simply seeks to emphasize that there is nothing more important and that there is no cost too great when it comes to the kingdom of God.

In the study of parables therefore we should seek the main point of the parable and not press its details. (This does not exclude the possibility that at times details in the picture part of a parable may refer to a corresponding reality. Cf. Mark 4:13–20; Luke 14:23; 20:15. Nevertheless, the greater danger for most interpreters is to see too much meaning in specific details rather than too little!)

It has been argued that we cannot translate the point of a parable into a nonparabolic statement. This is because when we do so, the powerful impact of the parable is lost. This objection is well taken. No one can deny that the parable of the good Samaritan (Luke 10:30–35) has more persuasive power than the summary "we should love our neighbor who is in need just like the good Samaritan loved the man who fell among thieves." Similarly, the parable of the prodigal son (Luke 15:11–32) impacts the reader far more forcefully than the statement "In this parable Jesus is defending his ministry among the outcasts of Israel and challenging the Pharisees and teachers of the law to enter into the joy of God's salvation coming to these outcasts."

The difference between a parable and the statement of its point lies, however, not in their meaning but in their ability to affect the reader or hearer. A parable consists of commissive language, whereas a statement of its meaning consists of referential language (see pp. 73–74). As a result the difference lies not with the meaning, which is the same for both, but rather in their differing ability to elicit response. If we redefine the meaning of a parable as consisting of both the willed pattern of meaning found in this literary and its power to affect response, then a restatement of the parable's meaning will always be inadequate. By definition it will always be inadequate because it lacks the persuasive dimension of commissive language. However, if meaning is primarily cognitive, involving the mind and understanding rather than the will and significance, then a parable's meaning can be restated as a "point" using referential language.

What Was the Point Jesus Sought to Make?

If "meaning" is determined by the author, we possess in the parables of Jesus two possible authors. One is, of course, Jesus, who created the parables; the other is the Evangelist who in his work interpreted Jesus' parables for his readers. Both have willed a meaning in telling the parable. (This should not be confused with those who argue that the parables are "polyvalent" and have multiple meanings, because

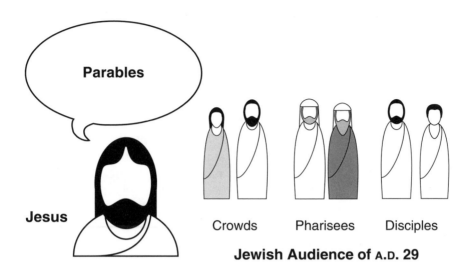

Parables

Jesus

Crowds   Pharisees   Disciples

Jewish Audience of A.D. **29**

the latter views these multiple meanings as a property of the text or of the reader.) Here we have two authors, Jesus and the Evangelist, who both will a meaning. These meanings, although possessing a similar pattern of meaning, tend to be addressed to different audiences and to emphasize different implications. When the parables are interpreted in the original setting, the situation of Jesus, they become exciting and alive. Instead of being viewed simply as timeless illustrations, they are now seen, as one writer has stated, as weapons of warfare with which Jesus battled his opponents.

This can be illustrated from the parable of the good Samaritan. Years ago when my daughter was about ten years old, I asked her to play a game with me. I asked her to answer my questions without reflecting on how she should answer. She was simply to tell me what immediately came into her mind. When she agreed, I said to her, "Samaritan." She responded with terms such as "good," "Jesus," "loving," "Christian," "hospital." When I said, "priest," the terms tended to be somewhat negative. Probably many, if not most, people would respond in a similar way, at least with respect to the term "Samaritan." The result is that for most people the parable of the good Samaritan is a pleasant tale of a good man who did a good deed whereas bad men did not.

On the other hand, if we could ask Jesus' audience to respond to these terms, they would respond very differently. For the Jews in Jesus' audience, the Samaritans were hated and cursed, and this attitude was mutual! They were so hated and despised that if people wanted to insult someone they could say, "Aren't we right in saying that you are a Samaritan and demon-possessed?" (John 8:48). Hatred between Samaritans and Jews had been festering for nearly a thousand years. Jews would have nothing to do with Samaritans (John 4:9). To speak of a "good Samaritan" was a contradiction in terms for Jesus' audience. It would be like talking about a square circle or a faithful adulterer. On the other hand, priests and Levites were thought of quite positively. Jesus purposely shaped his parable knowing that it clashed with the established values of his audience. As a result his parable is not a pleasant tale with expected results. On the contrary, it is a damning indictment directed against the social attitudes of his opponents. Their heroes are portrayed as villains and their villains as heroes.

Likewise when we interpret other parables in the setting of Jesus, they also take on a new life and vitality. The parables of the lost sheep (Luke 15:4–7), the lost coin (Luke 15:8–10), and the prodigal son (Luke 15:11–32) must be understood as addressed to those who "muttered, 'This man welcomes sinners and eats with them'" (Luke 15:2). Thus, the emphasis is not on the demonstration of God's love for the outcasts but on the reaction of the older brother to such love. If these parables were aimed at tax collectors and sinners (Luke 15:1), then their main point would be to illustrate God's great love toward them. But since the audience to which these parables were aimed were Pharisees and teachers of the law, the point is somewhat different. Jesus through these parables appealed to them, Why are you not rejoicing in what God is doing? (Luke 15:7, 10, 24, 32). The lost are being found; the lame walk; tax collectors and sinners are entering the kingdom. Why, like this older brother, can't you join in the banquet celebration? The parable of the workers in the vineyard (Matt. 20:1–16) makes the same point.

The second basic rule for interpreting the parables seeks the meaning of its original author. It can be stated as follows: seek the meaning of the parable that Jesus intended. The interpretation of any of Jesus' parables should, of course, be undertaken in the context of his entire teaching. It is important that a parable of the kingdom (the "part") should be interpreted in light of what Jesus says elsewhere on this subject (the "whole").

What Was the Point the Evangelist Sought to Make?

It has become increasingly clear that the Gospel writers were not simply recorders of the Jesus traditions but interpreters of them as well.

They believed that they were called of God not only to share the teachings and acts of the Son of God but to interpret them for their readers. It is not surprising therefore that we have four Gospels that are both similar and different. Each Evangelist felt free to explain, clarify, apply, abbreviate, or reorder these materials as the Spirit of God led them. In so doing they provided an inspired record and interpretation of the Jesus traditions for us.

On several occasions the Gospel writers took parables of Jesus aimed at one audience and applied the same pattern of meaning in the parable to a new situation. This was necessary because many of Jesus' para-

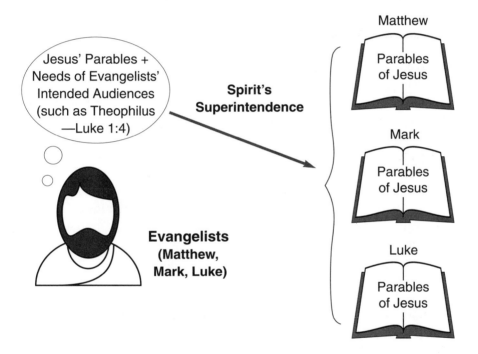

bles were addressed to such groups as the Pharisees and teachers of the law, and these people were not the audience to whom the Gospels were written. Thus Luke in writing to Theophilus (Luke 1:1–4) had to apply the parables and traditions of Jesus, which had originally been spoken to one audience, to a new audience. We find several examples of this in his Gospel. In the parable of the four soils, Luke applies this parable to the needs of his particular audience. In so doing he singles out certain dangers that they need to avoid (believing for only a time—8:13; the danger of riches and pleasure—8:14) and qualities that need to be nurtured (a good and noble heart, perseverance—8:15). These Lukan emphases can be seen most clearly by comparing them to the form of the parable found in Mark 4:3–20.

Another example of this is found in Luke 16:1–8 where we find a parable of Jesus that teaches the need for resolute action and decision. Originally this parable was probably directed to a different audience and involved the need to repent in light of the coming of the kingdom of God. It is now applied by Luke to the believing community, and other sayings of Jesus have been placed at this point. These sayings illustrate how Luke's readers can prepare for their time of accounting by a wise stewardship of their possessions (vv. 9–15).

Matthew also illustrates this principle in his version of the parable of the lost sheep (Matt. 18:12–14). Whereas the original audience consisted of Pharisees and teachers of the law (Luke 15:1–3, 4–7), Matthew applies the pattern of teaching found in this parable to his Christian audience (18:1, 5–6, 10, 14). As a result the problem sheep is not described as "lost" (Luke 15:4, 6) but as "wandering away" (Matt. 18:12–13), and the application or reality part involves the need of the Christian community to seek out the members, the "little ones," who are wandering away. They must be sought and brought back into the fold. Both the meaning of the parable willed by Jesus and that willed by Matthew involve the same pattern of meaning: God loves outcasts, whether inside or outside the believing community, and they should be sought and welcomed.

If the Evangelists have interpreted the parables in this manner, this means that they are now also authors of the parables. Thus, even as we have sought the meaning of the parable that Jesus intended we should also seek the meaning of the parable that the Evangelists intended.

Guidelines for Arriving at the Main Point

In seeking to arrive at the main point of the parable there are several questions that prove useful.

Who Are the Main Characters?

In parables in which several characters are found, there are always two or three characters who are most important. Usually it is quite easy to narrow down the multiple characters to three. For instance, in the parable of the prodigal son the three most important characters are

Parable of the Laborers in the Vineyard

   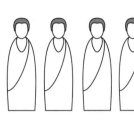

Landowner	First Hour Worker	Eleventh Hour Worker	3rd, 6th, 9th Hour Workers Steward

clearly the father, the prodigal son, and the older brother. In the parable of the laborers in the vineyard (Matt. 20:1–16) there are again three: the landowner, the first hour workers, and the eleventh hour workers. In the latter parable it is evident that the third, sixth, and ninth hour workers are unimportant because they do not appear later in the evening accounting. To ask the question, "Which two of these three characters are most important?" is helpful in drawing our attention to the particular characters Jesus and the Evangelists wanted to emphasize.

What Occurs at the End?

One author has referred to this guideline as "the rule of end-stress." It is based on the fact that good storytelling builds up and focuses interest on the conclusion of the story. A good mystery holds the reader in suspense until the very end when everything is explained and becomes clear. This is why we dare not miss the closing minutes of an episode in "Murder She Wrote," "Perry Mason," "Sherlock Holmes," or an Alfred Hitchcock movie. Even as a good comedian does not give away the punchline of a joke until the very end and a good mystery does not give away the solution until the end, so a good story builds up and concentrates the attention of the hearers on the final conclusion.

In a similar way a parable focuses its emphasis and point on the end of the story. The point of the parable of the workers in the vineyard (Matt. 20:1–16) would be very different if the conclusion read something like:

> When evening came, the owner of the vineyard said to his foreman, "Call the workers and pay them their wages, beginning with the first ones hired and going on to the last." The workers who were hired first came and each received a denarius. So when those came who were hired last, they expected to receive less. But each one of them also received a denarius. When they received it, they marveled and said of the landowner, "Truly this is a generous man."

If Jesus had told the parable in this manner, the focus would fall on the end action of generosity. The purpose of the parable would then be to illustrate that God is generous and kind. But Jesus did not teach the parable in this manner. He ended the parable with the grumbling of the first hour workers. This is where he wanted to focus his hearers' attention. The point of the parable for Jesus therefore centers on the reaction of the first hour workers. This picture part is emphasized because the reality to which Jesus was pointing involves the unwillingness of the Pharisees and teachers of the law to accept and rejoice in God's gracious offer of salvation to the lost. Similarly the focus of attention in the parable of the prodigal son is on the father and the older brother.

What Occurs in Direct Discourse?

If a parable contains a conversation, this requires the readers to focus their attention on what is being said. Thus, in the parable of the workers in the vineyard it should be noted that no conversation takes place between the landowner and the eleventh hour workers. Yet an extensive one takes place between the landowner and the first hour workers (Matt. 20:11–15). Similarly, there is no conversation between the father and the prodigal son. True, the son has his speech memorized and recites it (Luke 15:18–19, 21), but the father does not respond in any way. However, there is an extensive conversation between the father and his older son (vv. 29–32). In both instances Jesus wanted to focus his hearers' attention on this conversation.

Who Gets the Most Space?

Usually in telling a story we spend the most time describing the important characters. Minor characters receive minor attention; major characters receive major attention. In the parable of the workers in the vineyard it is evident by the amount of space devoted to the first hour workers (Matt. 20:1–2, 10–15) that they are more important than the eleventh hour workers (vv. 6–7, 9). This great discrepancy in space clearly indicates that the point of the parable lies with the first hour workers' response to the landowner. The issue is not as clear in the parable of the prodigal son. The space devoted to the prodigal involves thirteen verses (Luke 15:12–24) whereas the older brother is referred to in eight (vv. 25–32). This, however, is not sufficient reason to overlook the fact that the older brother appears at the end and that the only dialogue found in the parable involves him.

Conclusion

The key to interpreting the parables is to remember that they are not extended allegories but that they tend to teach a single basic point. We should therefore focus our attention on the basic analogy in the picture part and its corresponding point in the reality part. For example, in the parable of the prodigal son the analogy is that just as the older brother will not accept and rejoice in the loving forgiveness that his father has extended to his brother, so the Pharisees and teachers of the law are unwilling to accept God's loving forgiveness of tax collectors and sinners through the ministry of Jesus. This, however, does not make the parable an allegory, because there is present only a single basic analogy, and every metaphor or simile contains a basic analogy.

At times in the search for the basic point of the parable, the following questions prove helpful: Who are the two main characters? What comes at the end? Who is involved in a dialogue? To whom or what is the most space devoted? After having correctly understood the meaning of Jesus and/or the Evangelist, however, our task is not over. The most important aspect of interpretation still lies ahead. We must now seek those implications that are most relevant for us and act on them. What ultimately does it profit us, if we have learned the meaning of a parable without allowing that meaning and its implications to affect our lives?

Questions

1. Keeping in mind the definition of meaning in chapter 2, why must Augustine's interpretation of the parable of the good Samaritan be incorrect?
2. What is the difference between an allegory and a parable?

3. Read the parable of the laborers in the vineyard (Matt. 20:1–16) and compare it with the parable of the prodigal son (Luke 15:11–32). How are they alike?

4. To whom did Jesus address the parables of Luke 15:4–32? How does the audience to whom Jesus spoke affect our understanding of his main point? In other words, if these parables were addressed to "tax collectors and 'sinners'" (Luke 15:1) would the point be different than if he addressed them to "Pharisees and the teachers of the law" (Luke 15:2)?

11

The Game of Stories—
Biblical Narrative

The literary form found most frequently in the Bible is
narrative. Within the Judeo-Christian tradition this genre
of literature possesses unique importance. Many people first encounter
the Bible by means of its stories. These stories, whether of Joseph,
Moses, Samson, David, Isaiah, Jesus, or Paul, all involve biblical narrative. Vast sections of the Bible use this form. Over 40 percent of the
Old Testament and nearly 60 percent of the New Testament consist of
narrative. This involves such books as Genesis, Exodus, Joshua to Esther,
Matthew to Acts, and large portions of Numbers, Deuteronomy, and
the Prophets.

A great deal of effort has been spent recently on how this literary
form functions and how to interpret it. Unfortunately, much of the discussion is technical and often confusing. The discussion has also intro-
duced new terminology that the uninitiated find perplexing and incomprehensible. We tend to be overwhelmed when encountering such terms
as real author (the actual, historical person who wrote the work); implied
author (the author whom the reader can reconstruct from reading the
work); the narrator, sometimes defined as an overt or covert narrator
(the person who in the work relates the story but who may be unreli-
able and thus not the implied author); the omniscient and omnipresent
narrator (the person who in the work relates the story and is present

everywhere and knows everything [such as what people are thinking]); story world (the world created by the author in the work but which may not be real); point of view (the interpretation of the event by the author, i.e., the meaning of the author); intended reader (the reader whom the author had in mind when he wrote); real reader (anyone who reads the account); ideal reader (a reader who possesses sufficient information to interpret the account correctly).

In our discussion of biblical narrative we shall seek to simplify this terminology. We shall refer to the author and make no distinction between the real author and the implied author. Such a distinction is unnecessary as long as we realize that our knowledge and understanding of the author are imperfect and come from the text itself. An example of this is found in the four Gospels. All the Gospels are anonymous and make no overt claims as to authorship. (The present ascriptions "The Gospel of Matthew," "The Gospel of Mark," etc., date from the middle of the second century and stem from tradition, not from any claim made by the Gospels themselves.) When we refer to Matthew, Mark, Luke, and John, therefore, we mean the authors of the first, second, third, and fourth canonical Gospels and what we can know about them from these Gospels. Furthermore, since we can assume that the narrator of the biblical accounts is reliable and espouses the same viewpoint as the author, we shall make no distinction between them but treat these terms as synonymous.

The expression "story world" seems more appropriate in dealing with narratives that use the genre of myth. As we shall see, biblical narrative assumes a "this-worldly" framework of time and space, so that this expression is an unnecessary intrusion of issues of significance into the search for a text's meaning. As for "point of view," since the point of view in the story is that of the author/narrator, the expression is essentially a synonym for the "meaning" the author/narrator gave to the events he was reporting. Since the writer believed that he spoke for God, his point of view and God's point of view are the same. In the same way the writer's point of view in the Gospels is the same as Jesus' point of view. Being God's spokesman, the writer was not limited in place and time. He could thus express God's point of view and possessed a literary omnipresence (Gen. 3:1–24; Job 1:6–12; 2:1–6) and omniscience (Gen. 6:6, 8; 29:20; 38:15; 2 Sam. 11:27; Luke 2:29, 38; John 2:23; 4:1; Acts 24:26).

The Genre of Biblical Narrative—Myth or History?

During the first three millennia in which biblical narratives existed, interpreters all thought that they were historical accounts. Even those who applied an allegorical interpretation to these accounts acknowledged that the events were also literally true. Despite the presence of the miraculous in such accounts, the events portrayed in them were interpreted as having occurred in time and space. Interpreters believed that if one were present at the time when these events took place, they could have been observed just as described in the biblical narrative. In other words, interpreters of biblical narrative all assumed that this literary form was historical in nature. The closest analogy to this material would be reports of other historical events.

With the coming of the Enlightenment in the seventeenth and eighteenth centuries skepticism arose with regard to the supernatural. At first this skepticism was applied to pagan mythology and various church traditions, but it was not long before it was applied to the Bible. In England the deists began to question various kinds of biblical narratives containing miracles. Did an axehead really float (2 Kings 6:6)? Did the sun really stand still (Josh. 10:12–14)? It was not long until the historicity of all the miracles of the Bible began to be questioned.

As skepticism increased toward those biblical narratives that told of miraculous events, the issue arose as to how such narratives could be "meaningful" if they were not historically true. Previous to the Enlightenment the meaning of a text was sought by investigating the willed meaning of the author. This was accessible because the author intentionally conformed to the norms of language that governed the literary form he used. With respect to biblical narrative a literal, grammatical exegesis provided the meaning of the text. The historical subject matter being discussed was assumed to correspond with the meaning of the author. Yet what was to be done when someone no longer believed the miraculous subject matter of the biblical stories? It is interesting to note that for the most part the question was never raised as to whether these accounts were "meaningful," whether they possessed significance. Despite their supposedly fictional nature accounts of miracles were assumed to be meaningful. They had to be meaningful. This was a given. The close tie to the Christian church of many of those who denied the possibility of miracles simply did not permit the possibility that, since the meaning of the story involved a miracle, this meaning had no significance because the story was untrue. Thus, in order to preserve the "meaningfulness" of the biblical narratives, meaning had to be redefined and sought elsewhere than in the willed intention of the author. The meaning of the miracle stories in the Bible was to be found somewhere other than in what the author willed to convey.

Three alternatives presented themselves. The first was to seek the meaning in the event portrayed in the text. This was the approach of rationalism. Rationalists in the eighteenth and nineteenth centuries saw the meaning in the event reported in the text, but the event was different from its report. The literal description, which was miraculous, was not what actually took place. The present narrative is a fictional portrayal of the event. However, a real, nonsupernatural event lay behind this account, and discovering this was the goal of rationalism. One should therefore seek to reconstruct the event in order to find what really happened. Thus, what actually took place in the feeding of the five thousand was not a miraculous multiplication of loaves and fishes. Rather, it all started when a little boy was willing to share his few loaves and fishes. This caused others, who had brought more than enough, to share their food, and the result was that all the people were fed. Thus, the "meaning" of the biblical text was to be found in the reconstructed and "demiracalized" event. Whereas the reconstruction just given resulted in a "meaning" or point ("if people will only share what they have, there will be more than enough to go around"), most rationalistic reconstructions left the interpreter with little or nothing to preach or teach. What is the value of a misinterpreted event such as the sun shining through the clouds and illuminating Jesus and two men on a mountain? Where is there any meaningfulness in Jesus walking along the shore and being mistaken as walking on the sea?

The influence of rationalism was so great that even those who believed in the inspiration of the text shifted their attention away from the author's willed meaning and focused their attention on the subject matter of the event. Thus, what the author willed to teach by the event was lost sight of, and the event came to contain meaning in and of itself. The biblical stories as a result were treated independently of the literary context their authors gave them.

A second major attempt to find meaningfulness in the miracle stories of the Bible, while denying their facticity, was the theory of accommodation. According to this view, the authors of the biblical narratives knew that the events they were telling did not occur in the manner reported. They, like those proposing this theory, knew that no such miracles had occurred. But the authors realized that they were living among and seeking to minister to readers who believed in miracles and the presence of the supernatural in life. Thus, they shaped the principles and truths they sought to teach in the form of miracle stories. It should be noted, that according to the accommodationists, the meaning of these stories was what the authors willed to teach by them. However, the meaning was to be found in the willed meaning of authors who consciously presented myths that their readers would think were true for the purpose of teaching ideal truths and principles.

In comparing the rationalists and the accommodationists we find an interesting paradox. The rationalists, on the one hand, thought little of the intellectual ability of the biblical narrators, who badly misinterpreted what actually took place. The accommodationists, however, preserved the intellectual ability of the writers, for the writers were intelligent enough to know that these events were not true. Furthermore, they were brilliant in using the mythical mind-set of their readers to teach various religious principles. On the other hand, the rationalists protected the integrity of the biblical writers. They might not have been very smart, but they were honest! The accommodationists, while protecting the authors' intelligence, sacrificed their integrity. The biblical writers were quite dishonest, for they purposely misled their readers into thinking that what they were reporting was actually true. The view of the accommodationists also possessed a serious flaw in that they were never able to demonstrate that the biblical writers did not believe the historicity of what they were reporting. On the contrary, one thing that seemed reasonably clear to supernaturalists and nonsupernaturalists alike was that the biblical authors truly believed the facticity of what they were reporting.

The third major attempt to find meaning in biblical narratives that were miraculous was the mythical approach. Those who favored this view accepted the integrity of the authors and acknowledged that the biblical writers truly believed in the events they were reporting. They also referred to the authors' meaning by appealing to their inner consciousness that gave rise to the miracle stories—myths—that they reported. The biblical myths were essentially religious ideas dressed in historical clothing. The goal of interpretation was to discover the meaning of these myths, what is represented by these fictional accounts. This in turn was seen as the truth that was working in the subconsciousness of the authors as they wrote these myths. (This "subconsciousness" should not be confused with the "unconscious meaning" of an author's meaning, for unconscious meaning is a legitimate implication originating out of the consciously willed meaning of the author.) In the nineteenth century these subconscious meanings that were at work in the author tended to be good nineteenth-century liberal truths and values. In the first part of the twentieth century they tended to be existentialistic calls for decision.

The main problem with the mythical approach to biblical narrative is that it confuses historical issues and literary genre. If we leave aside the question of the facticity of the miracle stories in the Bible, the whole question of whether these stories are "myths" becomes extremely easy to answer. The biblical narratives are not myths. They do not possess a mythical literary form. The stories in the Bible are best described as "realistic narrative" in that they are straightforward and use the language of ordinary events. The biblical stories take for granted the world

Fables   ### Historical Narrative

Lucy found that she had come to the land of Narnia where it's always winter but never Christmas . . . Then she met Mr. Tumnus who was like a man from the waist up but had the legs of a goat and goat's hoofs . . . The white witch called herself the Queen of Narnia but all the Fauns and Dryads and Naiads and dwarfs and animals hated her. And she could turn people into stone! . . .

In the fifteenth year of the reign of Tiberus Caesar — when Pontius Pilate was governor of Judea, Herod . . . The word of God came to John, son of Zechariah . . . He went in all the country around the Jordan. For Jim and Alice December 7th was a quiet morning. They were eating dinner listening to the radio when they heard "We interrupt this program for a special announcement. The Japanese have bombed Pearl Harbor . . ." Immediately their lives were forever changed.

as we tend to experience it. Mythical monsters and places are not found in them. Real events are described involving real persons, in real places, at real times. The biblical narratives assume that what is depicted in them has in fact actually taken place. There is no difference between biblical narrative and history with respect to literary genre. To call the biblical stories "myths" is an incorrect genre description. To do so confuses a historical judgment such as "Miracles do not happen, so that the biblical narratives are untrue" with a literary one such as "Biblical narratives use the literary form of myth." To assess a biblical narrative as "mythical," therefore, has nothing to do with the literary form of the narrative and how we can ascertain what the author meant. It is rather a judgment of the facticity of the narrative, and this affects "significance" not "meaning." It is essentially a historical judgment using a literary rather than historical classification.

In the process of seeking to make the biblical narratives "meaningful," the rationalists, the accommodationists, and the mythicists were all seeking to find relevance in this form of biblical material. Yet the preoccupation with the facticity of the subject matter caused them to lose sight of where meaning is to be found. The meaning of a biblical narrative is to be found in what the author willed to teach his reader by recalling this incident. It is not found in some hypothetical subconsciousness of the biblical authors. Nor is it found in the event itself; it is not identical with its subject matter. This can be seen rather clearly if we seek to complete the following sentence, "I, Mark, have told you how one day Jesus was crossing the Sea of Galilee with his disciples when a great storm arose . . . because_____." We cannot fill in the blank by simply retelling the subject matter of Mark 4:35–41. Meaning is not simply retelling what happened. The "meaning" of Mark 4:35–41 involves what Mark is seeking to teach his readers by retelling this story.

Principles for Interpreting Biblical Narrative

The purpose of biblical narrative is not merely to tell what took place in the past. Rather, it is to relate these past events to biblical faith. Thus, the meaning of such texts involves not simply "what happened" but rather the interpretation of what happened. Unlike legal materials or letters, however, the meaning of a narrative is taught implicitly rather than explicitly. The writers of the biblical narratives seldom say, "Now the point I am trying to make by this story is . . ." Thus, the meaning of a narrative is more allusive for the reader. To facilitate the interpretation of biblical narrative, the following are especially useful.

Context

Since a biblical narrative is always part of a larger narrative, the author assumes that his readers will seek to discover the meaning of a particular narrative in light of the overall meaning of the book. This is a good example of what is known as the "hermeneutical circle." The reader in seeking to understand the part (the particular narrative) does so in light of an understanding of the whole (the entire book). In turn, this understanding of the part makes clearer the understanding of the whole. It is common sense to realize that we must interpret a chapter in a book in light of the rest of the book, and of course we interpret the whole book in light of its individual chapters. This whole process is both helpful and frustrating. It is frustrating in that it ultimately requires that the reader possess an understanding of the entire work to interpret correctly the particular narrative he or she is reading. It is helpful, however, because the author provides by his entire work a useful context for the reader to interpret each narrative.

Sometimes the immediate context provides a clue for how the author intends his readers to interpret the narrative. An example of this is found in Mark 1:2–8. In this passage Mark tells the story of Jesus' baptism by John the Baptist. Frequently this passage is read (and taught) as follows:

> It is written in Isaiah the prophet: "I will send *my messenger* ahead of you who will prepare your way"—"a *voice of one calling in the desert*, 'Prepare the way for the Lord, make straight paths for him.'" And so *John came, baptizing* in the desert region and preaching a baptism of repentance for the forgiveness of sins. The whole Judean countryside and all the people of Jerusalem went out *to him*. Confessing their sins, they were baptized *by him* in the Jordan River. *John* wore clothing made of camel's hair, with a leather belt around his waist, and *he ate* locust and wild honey. And this was *his message*: "After me will come one more powerful than I, the thongs of whose sandals I am not worthy to stoop down and untie. *I baptize* you with water, but he will baptize you with the Holy Spirit." (Mark 1:2–8; author's italics and underlining)

In the above passage the italicized words tend to receive the emphasis when read. If the passage is preached or taught, the speaker may spend time on such things as John's godly parents, his miraculous birth, where and when he ministered, or how he died. If the speaker had done some research about John the Baptist, he or she may share some information about John found in the works of Josephus, talk about the relationship of John's and Jewish proselyte baptism, or discuss John's possible relationship to the Qumran community that also had Isaiah 40:3 as its theme verse.

Yet Mark provides a context by which he wants his readers to interpret this narrative. His immediate contextual hint is found in Mark 1:1: "The beginning of the gospel about Jesus Christ, the Son of God." Although there is a textual question about whether the expression "the Son of God" was originally part of the Gospel of Mark, this context indicates that the meaning of the passage does not lie in the history of John the Baptist. No, in Mark's understanding, Mark 1:2–8 is a narrative about Jesus, not John! This narrative is told by Mark in order to help his readers know that Jesus is the Christ, the Son of God. John the Baptist has no importance for Mark in and of himself. He is valuable only because he helps Mark tell who Jesus is. Thus the emphasis in reading this passage should not be on the italicized words but on the underlined words. This narrative enables Mark to show that Jesus of Nazareth is the Promised One, the Christ, the Son of God. John is the person that the Old Testament promised would one day come to prepare for the Messiah and Lord. Jesus is that One. From the context that Mark provides in Mark 1:1, we know what the meaning of the present narrative is.

This is confirmed when we take into consideration the context of the entire book. The Gospel of Mark is a Gospel about Jesus. From Mark 1:1 to 16:8 Jesus is the focus of attention. There is no narrative in the book that does not in some way center on him. He is the main content, the focus, and the object of the entire Gospel. Thus, as we read Mark 1:2–8 we need to ask the question, "Why did Mark in telling us about Jesus include this story?" The larger context of the entire work also seeks to have us read this narrative in light of what it teaches about Jesus of Nazareth.

Another way in which an author gives clues as to how he wants his readers to interpret a narrative can be through his introductions and conclusions of the narrative. Deuteronomy ends with a conclusion that summarizes the books of Exodus through Deuteronomy:

Now Joshua son of Nun was filled with the spirit of wisdom because Moses had laid his hands on him. So the Israelites listened to him and did what the LORD had commanded Moses. Since then, no prophet has risen in Israel like Moses, whom the LORD knew face to face, who did all those miraculous signs and wonders the LORD sent him to do in Egypt— to Pharaoh and to all his officials and to his whole land. For no one has ever shown the mighty power or performed the awesome deeds that Moses did in the sight of all Israel. (34:9–12)

By this conclusion the author concludes the Pentateuch and introduces the Book of Joshua. Similarly, in Exodus 3:6–12 the author begins with an introduction that reveals what is to take place in Exodus through Deuteronomy.

The introduction to the Book of Joshua gives readers the theme of this book in the opening verses: "After the death of Moses the servant of the LORD, the LORD said to Joshua son of Nun, Moses' aide: 'Moses my servant is dead. Now then, you and all these people, get ready to cross the Jordan River into the land I am about to give to them—to the Israelites'" (1:1–2). Clearly we are to interpret this book recognizing that it is about the divinely ordained successor to Moses whom God would use to lead the children of Israel into the promised land.

In Judges the author also introduces us to the theme of his work in the opening verses: "After the death of Joshua, the Israelites asked the LORD, 'Who will be first to go up and fight for us against the Canaanites?' The LORD answered, 'Judah is to go; I have given the land into their hands'" (1:1–2). The author reveals to us that this book is about a period in which there was a leadership crisis in Israel. No leader existed to succeed Joshua. And the author drives this point home in the concluding verse of the work when he points out that "In those days Israel had no king; everyone did as he saw fit" (21:25). The future role of the tribe of Judah is also pointed out, for when Israel received her king, he would come from Judah.

The Gospel writers also assist their readers in reading their individual narratives in light of contextual clues given in their introductions and conclusions:

> Jesus did many other miraculous signs in the presence of his disciples, which are not recorded in this book. But these are written that you may believe that Jesus is the Christ, the Son of God, and that by believing you may have life in his name. (John 20:30–31)

> A record of the genealogy of Jesus Christ the son of David, the Son of Abraham . . . After Jesus was born in Bethlehem in Judea, during the time of King Herod . . . Then Jesus came from Galilee . . . Then Jesus was led by the Spirit. (Matt. 1:1; 2:1; 3:13; 4:1)

> Many have undertaken to draw up an account of the things that have been fulfilled among us, just as they were handed down to us by those who from the first were eyewitnesses and servants of the word. There-

fore, since I myself have carefully investigated everything from the beginning, it seemed good also to me to write an orderly account for you, most excellent Theophilus, so that you may know the certainty of the things you have been taught. (Luke 1:1–4)

Each Gospel writer seeks through his various narratives to tell his readers about Jesus. As a result, most narratives in the Gospels should be interpreted as dealing with the identity and mission of Jesus.

Yet there is also a larger context within which the biblical narratives are written. The writers of the historical narratives in 1 and 2 Samuel, 1 and 2 Kings, and 1 and 2 Chronicles build upon the content of the Pentateuch, Joshua, and Judges. They accept as normative what has happened and is taught in these books, and they expect their readers to be acquainted with them and also to accept them as such. In a similar way the New Testament writers build on the teachings of the Old Testament (Matt. 1:1; Mark 1:2–3; Rom. 1:2; 4:1–3; 9:1–5; Heb. 1:1–2; James 1:1; etc.).

Authorial Comments

On numerous occasions the authors of the biblical narratives intrude into accounts and give interpretative clues to their readers as to how they should interpret these narratives. A familiar example of this is found in the expression that a king did "what was right in God's eyes" (1 Kings 14:8; 15:5; 22:43; 2 Kings 10:30; 14:3; 15:3, 34; 18:3; 22:2; 2 Chron. 24:2; 25:2; 26:4; 29:2; 34:2). Frequently the writer also describes why a king did right in God's eyes and thus shares his value system with his readers. The authors of these books also reveal who did "evil in the eyes of the Lord" (1 Kings 11:6; 15:26, 34; 16:19, 25; 21:25; 22:52; 2 Kings 3:2; 8:18, 27; 13:2, 11; 15:9, 18, 24, 28; 21:2, 15–16, 20; 23:32, 37; 24:9, 19; 2 Chron. 12:14; 22:4; 33:2, 9; 36:5, 9, 12) and what this evil was.

Throughout the biblical narratives we find various insertions by the authors that are intended to help the reader. Mark in his Gospel frequently inserts such comments when foreign words appears in his account (5:41; 7:11, 34; 15:22, 34) or to help his readers understand the incident he is reporting (12:12, 18, 42; 14:1–2, 56; 15:7, 16, 42; cf. Gen. 13:6; 14:2; Judg. 13:16; 1 Sam. 9:9; 2 Sam. 13:18; 19:32). The latter he frequently introduces in the Greek text with a "for" (6:16, 20, 48, 50; 7:3–4; 9:6, 31–32; 11:13, 18, 32). At times the Evangelist also inserts an important theological comment in order to assist his readers in seeing the theological importance of the incident. In Mark 7:19 he adds "(In saying this, Jesus declared all foods 'clean.')" This enables the reader to understand that one of the implications of this incident is that it was no longer necessary to keep Jewish food regulations as to "kosher" or "unkosher." Another such insertion is found in Mark 8:35 where the Evangelist adds the term "gospel" to the saying (cf. the parallel sayings in Matt. 16:25 and Luke 9:24). Thus, he indicates that to lose one's life for Christ is to lose one's life for the sake of the gospel. Elsewhere Mark appeals directly to his readers to pay attention to what they are reading (13:14) and refers to members of his reading audience (15:21).

Another way in which a narrator provides clues to help his readers know the meaning of his narrative involves the use of summary statements he inserts within the text. After the account of the creation in Genesis 1:1–30 the narrator summarizes God's work: "God saw all that he had made, and it was very good" (v. 31). Such summaries are also found in the Gospels. After the opening description of Jesus' coming on the scene, Mark gives a summary that provides the reader with both a time frame and theme for the ministry of Jesus: "After John was put in prison, Jesus went into Galilee, proclaiming the good news of God. 'The time has come,' he said, 'The kingdom of God is near. Repent and believe the good news!'" (Mark 1:14–15). The theme of the coming of the kingdom of God (4:11, 26, 30; 9:1, 47; 10:14–15, 23–25; 12:34; 14:25; 15:43) and the preaching (1:4, 7, 38, 45; 3:14; 5:20; 6:12; 7:36; 13:10; 14:9) of the gospel is a constant emphasis in the following narratives. Later Mark provides another summary to help his readers understand that Jesus' death was both necessary and in accordance with the divine plan: "He [Jesus] then began to teach them that the Son of Man must suffer many things and be rejected by the elders, chief priests and teachers of the law, and that he must be killed and after three days rise again. He spoke [the word] plainly . . . and Peter took him aside and began to rebuke him" (8:31–32). The importance of this theme for Mark is seen in the fact that this summary is repeated time and time again (9:30–31; 10:32–34, 45). Luke likewise through his summaries points out the divine necessity of the various gospel events he records, especially the death of Jesus (9:22; 13:33; 17:25; 22:37; 24:7, 26–27, 44; Acts 17:3).

Repetition

Another way the author shares his meaning with the reader is by the repetition of key themes. The author of Judges, for example, reveals his purpose in writing through the constant repetition of two main themes. One involves Israel's cyclical experience of rebellion, retribution, repentance, and restoration. (See 3:7–9 for a succinct summary of this.) When Israel does "evil in the eyes of the Lord" (2:11–12; 3:7, 12; 4:1; 6:1; 10:6; 13:1), the Lord hands them over to their enemies (2:14; 3:8, 12; 4:2; 6:1; 10:7; 13:1). When Israel cries to the Lord (repents) (3:9, 15; 4:3; 6:6–7; 10:10, 12), God then delivers them (2:16, 18; 3:9, 15; 6:9; 10:12). Clearly the author of Judges seeks to teach his readers that sin leads to judgment, but that repentance leads to salvation.

A further example of repetition by which the author of Judges helps his readers understand his work is found in the constantly repeated phrase "In those days Israel had no king" (17:6; 18:1; 19:1; 21:25). The author points out that the result of this is that chaos and anarchy reigned in Israel. At times God raised a deliverer or judge to rescue various tribes from their enemies, but the result of lacking a divinely ordained line of kings is that "everyone did as he saw fit" (17:6; 21:25). The author ends his work with these words and thus prepares his readers for the coming of God's gift of the monarchy. Note also how the biblical writers reveal God's sovereign rule over events by the repetition of the phrase "fulfilling the word the LORD had spoken" (1 Kings 2:27; 12:15; 15:29; 16:12, 34; 2 Kings 1:17; 23:16; 24:2).

We find a similar kind of repetition of key themes in the Gospel of Luke. Luke continually emphasizes the importance of the Holy Spirit in the life and ministry of Jesus. The Spirit is involved in the birth of John the Baptist (1:15) and the conception of Jesus (1:35). Before his birth the Spirit bears witness to Jesus (1:41–45). At his baptism Jesus is anointed by the Spirit in a powerful way (3:22—note "in bodily form like a dove"). "Full of the Spirit" he is then led by the Spirit into the wilderness (4:1). When he returns in the "power of the Spirit" to Nazareth (4:14), he announces in his first sermon, "The Spirit of the Lord is on me" (4:18). Clearly by this repetition Luke wants his readers to understand the importance of the Spirit in the life and ministry of Jesus, and this prepares for the importance of the Spirit for the life and ministry of the church in his second work, Acts.

Authoritative Speakers

Another way in which an author helps his readers understand the meaning of his narrative is by placing key dialogues in the mouths of various speakers. The reader knows, because of who is speaking, whether what is being said represents the mind of the narrator. For instance, when God or Jesus speaks, the reader knows that the author wants him or her to accept what is being said as true. Similarly, when faithful servants of God, such as a patriarch, prophet, or apostle speaks, this, too, can be relied upon as being true and authoritative, unless the narrator reveals otherwise. At times various characters are portrayed positively by the narrator, and the reader thus recognizes that what they say or do is to be accepted as being in accordance with the will of God. For example, Luke goes out of his way to describe Joseph of Arimathea as "a good and upright man . . . waiting for the kingdom of God"(Luke 23:50–51). Because he was a member of the Council that had plotted against Jesus, Luke also adds that he "had not consented to their decision and action." Thus, we can accept his action in burying Jesus as being good and noble. When Luke describes Zechariah and Elizabeth as being childless (Luke 1:7), since this might be misinterpreted as a sign of judgment upon them (cf. Gen. 16:4, 11; 29:32; 30:1; Lev. 20:20–21; 1 Sam. 1:5–6, 11; 2:5–8; 2 Sam. 6:23; Jer. 22:30; 36:30; Luke 1:25), he points out that they "were upright in the sight of God, observing all the Lord's commandments and regulations blamelessly" (Luke 1:6). Thus, we can rely on them as positive examples of piety except, as Luke points out, for Zechariah's momentary lack of faith (Luke 1:11–20).

Throughout the Bible the narrators help the reader understand how to interpret their words. This is often done through the use of positive characters (1 Sam. 29:9; 2 Sam. 14:17, 20; 19:27; 1 Kings 18:31; Job 1:1), but it is also done through evil characters (Gen. 13:13; 1 Sam. 2:12; 25:3; 2 Sam. 20:1; 1 Kings 12:8). The latter, of course, provide counsel and actions that are to be avoided. Even if an author does not provide an editorial description of these characters, we are able to judge whether he approves or disapproves of them according to whether they exemplify the character and plan of God revealed in the rest of the Bible. Even apart from any editorial comment, the reader knows whether they are to be viewed positively or negatively due to the teachings found in the earlier canonical writings. Similarly, unless they inform their readers otherwise, the authors assume that the actions, teachings, and behavior of the characters in the Gospels and Acts are to be interpreted positively or negatively in light of the teachings found in the Old Testament.

Dialogue or Direct Discourse

Within an account one way in which a narrator focuses the attention of his readers is by the use of dialogue. When indirect discourse (conversation reported indirectly) turns to direct discourse (conversation denoted by quotation marks) this is a clue that careful attention should be paid to what is being said. Thus, in the story of Jesus' stilling the storm the key for understanding the narrative comes in the words uttered by the disciples, "Who is this? Even the wind and the waves obey him!" (Mark 4:41). What Mark seeks to share with his readers as he recounts this tradition is that Jesus is the Christ, the Son of God. He is Master of nature itself. Even the dangers and threats of nature cannot overwhelm those who are his children!

Within various accounts we come across dialogues between God and his servants, and within those dialogues the major theme of the narratives becomes clear. It is in the divine theophany in Exodus 3, in which God directly speaks to Moses, that the author provides the clue for understanding both this narrative and the entire book. This narrative and book is about the One who said to Moses, "I am the God of your father, the God of Abraham, the God of Isaac and the God of Jacob. . . . I have indeed seen the misery of my people in Egypt. . . . So I have come down to rescue them from the hand of the Egyptians and to bring them up out of that land into a good and spacious land, a land flowing with milk and honey" (vv. 6–8). Within this narrative the direct discourse tells us that Moses would be used of God to lead the people of Israel out of their bondage to the Pharaoh of Egypt and ultimately into the land of Canaan. Similarly, in the opening discourse of Joshua 1:2–9 where the Lord speaks to Joshua the author sets the tone for not just the following narrative but the entire book.

Conclusion

The interpretation of biblical narrative presents some unique problems. This is especially true if the historicity of the events recorded in them is denied. If, however, the meaning of a biblical narrative is determined by what the author willed to say by it, then the historicity or lack of historicity of the event recorded in it does not in any way change the meaning of the account. The account means what the author willed to say by the account, whether the event described in it is true or untrue. To be sure, the significance of that meaning will radically change. Paul understood this. The interpretation that Paul gave to the death and resurrection of Jesus will always remain the same, regardless of whether Jesus rose from the dead or not. But if Christ did not rise from the dead, the interpretation Paul gave to it is foolish. It is a falsehood, and faith in this fictional story is futile (1 Cor. 15:12–19). Evangelical Christianity stands or falls on the facticity of the biblical narratives. It cannot seek for meaning in some mythical subconsciousness of the authors that gave birth to these fictions. Even less can it seek for meaning in a reconstruction of "what really happened." The meaning of a biblical narrative is what the author meant to teach by the event recorded in it. Since that meaning depended in their minds on the facticity of what they were reporting, if we do not believe these events occurred, the meaning must be rejected. It cannot, however, be changed into something else.

As for discovering that meaning, we have observed several principles that will assist us. The literary context that the author has given is most valuable. This context involves not just the verses that precede and follow the passage but the entire work within which the author has placed it. We must interpret a particular narrative in light of the theme and purpose of the entire book in which it is found. This requires study, but that study will be rewarded with a clearer understanding of how this particular narrative (part) fits into the entire book (whole). At other times the author assists his readers in the interpretation of his narrative by inserting various comments into the account. These may provide historical or cultural information needed to help understand the narrative. At times an author may provide a summary of some sort, and this can appear not just at the end of the narrative but at the beginning or in the middle as well. Through repetition an author also helps the reader understand what he sought to teach. Another way of assisting the reader is by the use of authoritative speakers who represent the point he is making. Likewise by his use of dialogue an author helps his readers focus in on the importance of what is being said. Keeping all this in mind, we can understand the meaning of a biblical narrative as long as we do not confuse this meaning with its subject matter. We will be assisted in this, if, as we investigate such narratives, we seek to fill in the following paradigm: "I [the biblical author] have written how that . . . [the biblical narrative] because_____."

Questions

1. What are some indications that a biblical author gives to indicate for readers that what follows is a parable; a historical narrative; a fable?

2. What is the main difference between a historical narrative like Shakespeare's *Julius Caesar* or Margaret Mitchell's *Gone with the Wind* and Winston Churchill's *The Second World War* or Cornelius Ryan's *The Longest Day?*

3. When reading a book to which parts should we pay particular attention in order to understand the author's purpose? What about a biblical book?

4. Why did/do many interpreters of biblical narrative reject the definition of meaning given in chapter 2?

5. Define what is meant by "context" in this chapter.

6. How would you interpret a work beginning "Once upon a time . . . "? How would you interpret a work beginning "It was early on the morning of June 6, 1944. A small ship secretly landed on the shores of Normandy when . . . "? Would you look for the "meaning" differently? What would be different? Would you treat the "significance" differently? The "subject matter"?

12

The Game of Correspondence—Epistles

In the New Testament the dominant literary form is the epistle or letter. Technically a "letter" is a less literary and more personal form of communication that tends to address a specific situation or problem and builds on an established relationship. An "epistle" is more artistic in form and is intended as a self-explanatory treatise to a wider public. The distinction between them can be blurred, however. Paul's writings seem to lie somewhere in between, with Philemon resembling a letter and Romans an epistle. Even as letters today possess a particular literary form (date; address; salutation; body; conclusion; name), so letters in biblical times also possessed a general form.

The Form of an Ancient Letter

Within ancient letters we usually find the following:

- Salutation—This consists of a reference to the sender ("Paul and Timothy, servants of Christ Jesus") and the recipient of the letter ("To all the saints in Christ Jesus at Philippi, together with the overseers and deacons") along with a greeting ("Grace and peace to you from God our Father and the Lord Jesus Christ"—Phil. 1:1–2). The Pauline salutation conforms to the conventions of his day. The main difference is that whereas the more traditional greeting of the time would use "Greeting" *(chairein)* as in Acts 15:23; 23:26; and James 1:1 and a Jewish greeting would use "Peace" *(shalom)*, Paul uses a more distinctly Christian greeting "Grace and peace." (In 1 Tim. 1:2 and 2 Tim. 1:2 we find "Grace, mercy, and peace.") On several occasions Paul uses his salutation to explain why he has written the letter (Rom. 1:5–7a; cf. 15:15–29) and to prepare his readers for his argument in the body of the letter (Gal. 1:4; cf. 1:11–2:21).

- Thanksgiving and/or Prayer—This is found in all Paul's letters except Galatians, where its omission is significant.

- Body—This is frequently the largest part of a Pauline letter as can be seen from Romans 1:18–11:36; Galatians 1:6–4:31; cf. also 1 Corinthians 1:10–4:21.

- Exhortation and Instruction—Note Romans 12:1–15:32; 1 Corinthians 5:1–16:18; Galatians 5:1–6:15.

- Conclusion—This can include such things as: a wish for peace (Rom. 15:33; 2 Cor. 13:11; Gal. 6:16); greeting (Rom. 16:1–15; 1 Cor. 16:1–20a; 2 Cor. 13:13); kiss (Rom. 16:16; 1 Cor. 16:20b; 2 Cor. 13:12); a concluding autograph (1 Cor. 16:21; Gal. 6:11; Col. 4:18; 2 Thess. 3:17); and benediction (Rom 16:20; 1 Cor 16:23–24; 2 Cor 13:14; Gal 6:18).

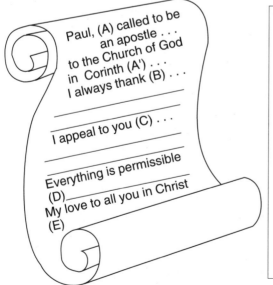

Paul, (A) called to be an apostle . . . to the Church of God in Corinth (A') . . . I always thank (B) . . .

I appeal to you (C) . . .

Everything is permissible (D) My love to all you in Christ (E)

April 1, 1994

Dear Joan, (A')

It was good hearing from you. I am glad that everything is going well (B) . . .

Let me share with you some of the things that have been happening (C) . . .

Don't be discouraged but keep looking up (D) . . .

Love, (E)

Bob (A)

An author was not enslaved to this form, but it is usually important for the interpreter to note those instances when the author chose to deviate from it. In Galatians Paul omits of a word of thanksgiving and/or prayer (b.) and thus reveals his anger and frustration over what was happening in the church. Paul simply could not find anything to be thankful about by the recent turn of events. At times Paul also used the thanksgiving to prepare his readers for what he was about to write in the body and exhortation of the letter. In 1 Corinthians 1:5 he refers to the "knowledge," "speaking," and "spiritual gifts" of the Corinthian church, and these are dealt with at length in 1 Corinthians 1:18–4:21 and 12:1–14:40. We can also see this in the thanksgiving in Philippians 1:4 (the theme of "joy") and 1:5 (the "partnership" of the Philippians and Paul in the gospel). The latter is referred to in 2:19–30; 4:10–19, and the former is found scattered throughout the letter (1:18, 25; 2:2, 17–18, 28–29; 3:1; 4:1, 4, 10). The unusual addition of material such as Galatians 1:1b–d and Romans 1:1b–6 to the salutation likewise reveals a great deal about the purpose of Paul in writing these letters.

In a similar way Paul at times uses his conclusions (e.) as an opportunity to recapitulate the material in the body (c.) and exhortation (d.) of his letter. This can be seen in Galatians 6:16 where he qualifies his normal benediction (cf. Rom. 15:33; 2 Cor. 13:11; Phil. 4:9; 1 Thess. 5:23; 2 Thess. 3:16) and in 6:17 where he summarizes the defense of his apostleship (cf. 1:11–2:21). Another example of this can be seen in 1 Thessalonians 5:23–24 where we have an exhortation to holy living (5:23a; cf. 1:3; 3:11–13; 4:1, 3–7; 5:8), a reference to Christ's return (5:23b; cf. 1:3, 10; 2:19; 3:13; 4:13–18; 5:1–11), and perhaps a call for faithfulness in times of persecution (5:24; cf. 1:6; 2:2, 14; 3:2–4).

Understanding the Words of Scripture

In seeking to understand how an author like Paul used a particular word, we can assume, unless stated otherwise, that the meaning he intended lies within the language norms of his audience (see above pp. 54–55). Thus, we can know the range of possible meanings of these words. This range of possibilities is available to us today in a Bible dictionary or, for those with facility in the biblical languages, in a Hebrew or Greek lexicon. The issue for the interpreter is how to narrow down these possibilities to the particular meaning of the word that the author intends for his readers to understand. (Although on rare occasions an author may intend a double meaning as in a pun, such occurrences are quite unusual.)

It is obvious that not all words are equally important in an author's argument. Some play a more critical role. For instance, the term "credit" ("reckon" in the RSV) is clearly a key term in Romans 4 due to its frequency (it occurs eleven times). At times an author helps his readers by carefully defining what he means by a particular term. This can be done in several ways. One of the most common is by the use of an explanatory clause. (Note how Paul explains what he means by the term "gospel" in 1 Cor. 15:1 by the "for" clause in vv. 3–5. Cf. also the explanation of "temple" in John 2:21; "mature" in Heb. 5:14 [cf. RSV]; "chief servant" in Gen. 24:2.) Another way an author explains the meaning of a term is by using an appositive (cf. "circumcision" in Rom. 4:11; "sexual immorality" in 1 Cor. 5:1). Still another way is by means of synonymous parallelism (cf. how "love" and "enemies" are explained by the parallelism in Luke 6:27–28; how "ask" and "being given" are explained in Matt. 7:7–8). In most instances, however, the specific meaning of a term must be ascertained in other ways.

The Value of Etymology

In the past interpreters have frequently investigated the etymology of a word in order to understand its meaning in a sentence. No doubt most of you have heard someone refer to the "root meaning of this word." I have personally heard someone elucidate the meaning of a biblical word by appealing to the root meaning of the English word used in translation! Apparently the speaker did not realize or reflect upon the fact that the biblical author did not write in English and that the English language did not exist at the time!

The fallacy of seeking to discover the particular meaning of a word by means of its etymology can be seen by reflecting on how we use language. When in the last twenty-four hours (or even week or month) have you thought of the etymology of any of the words that you use in speaking or writing? When we speak or write, we are almost always concerned with only the present meaning of the words we are using. In other words, we are not interested in what these words meant when they came into existence, but in what they mean now. Does anyone today when they use the term "nice" do so in light of the fact that in the eighteenth century it meant "precise" or that it comes from the Latin *nescius*, which means "ignorant"? Of course not. Or does anyone when they use the term "let" do so because it comes from an old Dutch word *lette*, which means to "hinder"? Not today, but the King James translators did in Romans 1:13 when they wrote "Now I would not have you ignorant brethren, that oftentime I purposed to come unto you, (but was "let" hitherto) . . . " Even when we use the term in this old sense in calling a tennis serve a "let," very few people think that we are using the verb "let" according to its old etymological meaning. (Two other examples of words whose root meanings are quite different are "generous" from the Latin *generosus*, which means "birth, race, class" and "asbestos" from the Greek *asbestos*, which means "inextinguishable.")

The etymology of a word is of little value in biblical interpretation. It is only useful in two instances. One is in those instances when we have no, or little, idea of what a biblical word means because it is found very seldom, or not at all, elsewhere. An example of this involves the word "daily" in the Lord's Prayer. This Greek term is found only three times in ancient Greek literature. (Someone has claimed to have found a fourth instance in a papyrus fragment, but this fragment cannot be found.) The three instances are in the Lord's Prayer in Matthew, the Lord's Prayer in Luke, and the Lord's Prayer in a early work called the Didache! In desperation scholars have referred to the possible root meaning of this word. We also find instances in the Old Testament in which a word is found only once or twice and nowhere else in the literature of the ancient Near East, and we do not know what it means. In such instances we are appealing again to a hypothetical etymological meaning because we have nothing else to go on. We are desperate! In all such instances we must be aware that we are essentially grasping at straws, and we should never place any great weight on this hypothetical meaning.

The second instance in which etymology appears to be useful is in the use of names. Frequently names were intentionally chosen because of the root meaning of the term. The most famous example of this is found in Matthew 1:21 where Joseph is told to give Mary's baby "the name Jesus [Heb. *yehoshua*], because he will save [Heb. *yeshua*] his people from their sins." The name given to Mary's son is carefully chosen based on the etymology of the name. "Jesus," which is the Greek equivalent of the Hebrew "Joshua," has as its root meaning "Yahweh is salvation." Two verses later in Matthew, Mary's son is called "Immanuel," which has as its root "God is with us." We find numerous instances in which Old Testament people are carefully named due to the etymology of the name. This was because of the common idea that people were/would be as they were named: Genesis 3:20 ("Eve"); 4:1–2 ("Cain"), 25 ("Seth"); 17:5 ("Abraham"); 21:3 ("Isaac"); 25:25 ("Esau"), 26 ("Jacob"); Hosea 1:9 ("Lo-Ammi"). Sometimes the name has etymological significance but is not explained as in: Elijah (YHWH is God); Shemaiah (The Lord has heard [the prayer of his parents]); Eliezer (My God is my help). The importance of etymology in names is seen especially in the names of God: Yahweh or LORD ("I am" or "I cause to be"); El Shaddai or the Almighty ("God Almighty"); El Elyon or the Most High ("God Most High"); El Olam or the everlasting God ("God of Eternity"); El Berith ("God of the Covenant"). Outside of these rather limited uses, however, the etymology of a word provides little assistance in understanding what an author means by the words he uses. This is especially true in those instances in which words have taken on an idiomatic meaning.

Understanding the Meaning by Means of Similar Authors

If the key resource for obtaining the possible meanings of a particular word is a dictionary or lexicon, the key resource for understanding its specific meaning is a concordance. By seeing how this word is used elsewhere, we can eventually come to understand how the author is using it in the particular instance we are studying. What do people who think like this author mean when they use this term? Who are the people who think most like this biblical author and what do they mean when they use this term? It is evident that Paul thought more like classical Greek writers than contemporary writers, even contemporary Greek writers. Thus when Paul in Ephesians 5:18 refers to "wine," it is probable that he thought more like ancient writers in their understanding of this word than like people today who use this word. Thus, it is probable that Paul meant by this word the same mixture of water and what we today call "wine" that the ancient Greek writers did (Homer, *Odyssey* 9.208–9; Pliny, *Natural History* 14.6.54; Plutarch, *Symposiacs* 3.9; and especially Athenaeus, *Learned Banquet*, Book 10).

We can come even closer to what Paul meant by asking how the writers of the Greek Old Testament (the Septuagint or LXX) understood a term, for Paul thought more like them than the Greek classical writers. In addition, since the Septuagint was the Bible of his churches, Paul would tend to use his words in a manner similar to how they were used in his readers' Bible. Even more helpful would be to understand how Paul's contemporaries, who wrote the other books of the New Testament, understood this term. More helpful still would be to find how the same author uses this term elsewhere in his letters. For instance, when Paul says in Philippians 1:29, "For it has been granted to you on behalf of Christ not only to believe on him, but also to suffer for him," his use of the term "granted" elsewhere sheds light on what he means here. The Greek term Paul uses is *echaristhē*. When Paul speaks of the grace of God and being saved by grace, he uses the noun form (*charis*) of this verb. Thus, when Paul speaks of suffering in Philippians 1:29, he is not speaking of something that a Christian may be forced to bear, or something that he is obligated to endure. On the contrary, suffering for Christ is a gracious privilege! Christians, Paul says, may be "graced" with the privilege of suffering for Christ. Clearly, understanding how Paul uses this word and its noun form elsewhere is helpful in understanding how he is using it here.

We also receive help in understanding what Paul means in Philippians 2:12 when he says "continue to work out your salvation with fear and trembling" by comparing how he uses this term "work out" elsewhere. This is not the term Paul uses in his discussion of justification by faith when he seeks to establish that justification is not by works. There Paul uses the noun *ergon* and the verb *ergazomai*. Here he uses the verb *katergazomai*, which appears a total of twenty times in Paul's letters. In none of these twenty instances, however, is there present any idea of meriting or earning something. The sense in which Paul uses this term can be seen in the following two passages:

> The things that mark an apostle—signs, wonders and miracles—were done among you with great perseverance. (2 Cor. 12:12)

> I will not venture to speak of anything except what Christ has accomplished through me in leading the Gentiles to obey God by what I have said and done. (Rom. 15:18).

The verbs "done" and "accomplished" are the same word Paul uses in Philippians 2:12. In these two examples it is clear that Paul is not speaking about meriting or earning anything. The signs of an apostle were not earned by Paul but were "manifested" or "demonstrated." Likewise, Christ did not earn or merit the salvation of the Gentiles through

Paul's preaching. From Paul's use of the term in these and other instances it is apparent that we should not interpret it to mean in Philippians 2:12 "Earn, work for, your salvation" but rather "Manifest, carry out the implications of the salvation which you already possess."

There are times when we can ascertain the particular meaning of a word by comparing how the author uses the term within the same book. We already saw an example of this when we discussed the meaning of the word "foolishness" in 1 Corinthians 2:14. It was evident from the way that Paul uses the same term in 1 Corinthians 1:20 and 3:19 that by "foolishness" he meant "rejected as foolish" and not "incomprehensible" or "incapable of being understood" (see above pp. 65–67). Another example of this is the meaning of the term "justification" in Romans. Much has been written on the subject but from Romans 8:33–34 it is evident that justification is the opposite of condemnation and from Romans 4:6–7 that it involves forgiveness.

Another example of how this works is found in the parable of the sheep and the goats in Matthew 25:31–46. The key issue in this account involves how we are to understand the expression "these brothers of mine" or "my brethren" (RSV) found in verse 40. Does Matthew by this term refer to the needy of the world, whether they are believers or not? Does he refer to fellow believers? Or does he refer here to the disciples and early missionaries of the church? Within the New Testament the expression "my brothers" or "my brethren" was frequently used as a description of the believing community (Acts 1:15–16; 15:13; Rom. 1:13; 7:1, 4; 1 Cor. 1:10–11; etc.). Far more valuable for understanding what this expression means is the fact that Matthew uses this same expression metaphorically four other times in his Gospel—12:48–50 (here it is used in the singular) and 28:10 (cf. v. 8)—and that in each of these instances it refers to the disciples. It is most likely therefore that it refers to them in 25:40 as well.

This is supported by the fact that the best analogy to this parable in the Gospel is found in 10:40–42 where the Christian community is told that receiving "these little ones" (cf. 10:42 with 25:40 "least of these brothers of mine") means receiving Jesus (cf. 10:40 with 25:35–40). (Cf. also the giving of "a cup of cold water" [10:42] with "I was thirsty and you gave me something to drink" [25:35, 37].) Thus, from Matthew itself we find sufficient evidence to conclude that the expression "these brothers of mine" refers to the apostles and early missionaries of the church. The reason why rejection of them is so serious is that they are Jesus' messengers, and to reject his messengers is to reject him. One's attitude toward the Gospel is clearly seen and reflected in how one treats those who proclaim the gospel. We need only compare the different treatment Paul received from the Philippian jailor before his acceptance of the gospel (Acts 16:23–24) and after (vv. 30–34). (Cf. also how Luke reveals what he means by the term "brought up" in Acts 22:3 by how he uses this same term in Acts 7:20, 26. [In the NIV "cared for" and "brought up" translate this same term.])

There are times that the meaning of a word becomes clear through the very paragraph in which it is found. There has been a great deal of confusion as to how James 2:14–26 can be reconciled with Paul's explicit teachings that justification is not by works but by grace alone. Within the norms of language these two terms can mean several things. If we investigate what James and Paul mean by the terms "faith" and "works," it becomes evident that they are not referring to the same thing. The faith that cannot save is described by James as: a faith that "had no deeds" (2:14); a faith that can ignore the naked and hungry in the believing community (vv. 15–16); a dead faith unaccompanied by good deeds (vv. 17, 26); an intellectual faith that believes a fact such as there being one God (v. 19a); and a faith that even demons can possess (v. 19b). James himself reveals that he does not accept this kind of mental assent as true faith when he says in 2:14, "Can such a faith save him?" Note that he does not say, "Can faith save him?" but rather "Can the kind of faith I just described, a faith that has no subsequent good deeds, save him?" The answer, of course, must be "No, that kind of faith, which even the demons have cannot save." Within the norms of language the term "faith" means for James mere mental assent, such as even demons possess. Demons know, they mentally accept, they "believe" in the sense in which the word is used in James 2:14–26. Yet the "faith" that Paul talks about is not mere mental assent but wholehearted trust and dependence on God and his saving grace. It is a "faith expressing itself through love" (Gal. 5:6).

As to what James means by "works," this is also different from what Paul means. For Paul, works cause boasting, "earn" favor, and place God in one's debt (Rom. 4:2–4). In Romans and Galatians they involve "works of law" and have as their focal point the Gentiles being circumcised, keeping the Sabbath and religious days of Judaism, and becoming kosher. It is focused on what we would today call ritualistic rather than ethical issues. On the other hand, when James speaks of works he refers to clothing the naked and feeding the hungry (2:15–16). Works reveal a person's faith (v. 18) and involve obedience to God, as in the case of Abraham (vv. 21–23) and Rahab (v. 25). They are faith's loving response to the needs of others. They are the natural and necessary result of faith's desire to please God. It is evident that the paragraphs in which James and Paul use the terms "faith" and "works" assist the reader to understand exactly what they meant by these terms.

Several additional examples in which insight into the meaning of a term is found in the immediate context are as follows: the term "gospel" in 1 Corinthians 15:1–2 is explained in verses 3–8; "justifies" in Romans 8:33 is shown to be the opposite of "condemns" in verse 34; what Jesus meant by "temple" in John 2:19–20 is explained by the Evangelist in verse 21 who also explains in 7:39 what Jesus meant by "streams of living water" in the previous verse; "credited to him as righteousness" ("reckoned righteous" RSV) in Romans 4:2 and 6 is explained in verses 7–8. Sometimes the explanation of a term can be found within the sentence itself. An example of this is found in Hebrews 5:14 where the author explains what he means by "mature" by the following relative clause. (Cf. also how in Gen. 24:3 "chief servant" is explained in the same verse and how in Rom. 4:11 the expression "sign of circumcision" is explained by the following appositive.)

Understanding the Propositions of Scripture

Words in isolation cannot possess specific meaning. It is only within sentences that they possess specific meanings. Whereas the first step in seeking to know the meaning of a biblical text involves knowing the meaning of the individual words (the "parts"), the next is to observe how these words function within the sentence (the "whole"). (Actually, the procedure is not as simple as this, for we cannot understand the specific meaning of a word without simultaneously understanding the meaning of the sentence in which it is found. This is another example of the hermeneutical circle.) Whereas the key tools for understanding what "words" mean are a dictionary/lexicon and a concordance, the key tool for understanding the meaning of a sentence is a grammar.

For the reader of an English translation of the Bible, this means that he or she must have the same understanding of English grammar that the translators possessed. For those who possess the ability to read the Hebrew Old Testament or the Greek New Testament, this means that they must possess knowledge of the grammar, the "syntax," of the biblical languages. It goes without saying that, because grammar changes, we must be sure that we are dealing with the same grammatical rules that the translators or authors worked with at the time. In interpreting the works of Paul, we must know the grammatical rules not of classical Greek or modern Greek but of the Greek that Paul and his readers shared in common, called "koine Greek." Similarly, when seeking to understand the King James Version we must know sixteenth- and early seventeenth-century English grammar, whereas in interpreting the New International Version we must know the middle-class English grammar of Americans during the 1970s and 1980s.

A sentence consists of a combination of words ("verbal symbols") used by their author to make some sort of a statement. When strung together, these sentences make up an argument. To decipher what the author meant by the sentence we must know how the words within them relate to each other. In English, word order is most important. The words "Bob loves Joan" in any other order ("Joan loves Bob," "Loves Bob Joan," "Loves Joan Bob," "Bob, Joan loves," "Joan, Bob loves") carry a different meaning. In Greek, however, word order plays a lesser role because the endings on the word determine which is the subject and which is the object. Thus, we can have: "Bob*us* agapei (loves) Joan*ēn*" or "Joan*ēn* agapei (loves) Bob*us*" and there is no real difference. Both mean "Bob loves Joan."

In the interpretation of the Bible readers often pay insufficient attention to how parts of sentences and clauses relate to one another. For example, the relationship between (1) "You are saved" and (2) "faith" will be radically altered if we use various words such as "because of," "before," "after," "despite," "since," "apart from," "regardless of," or "for." Most readers of the Bible pay far too little attention as to how such phrases and clauses relate to each other. The following is a description of some of the ways in which parts of sentences can relate to each other.

1. Cause—In this relationship (A) is because of (B), that is, (B) is the cause of (A): "The man died (A) *because* of his wounds (B)." Some of the terms used to describe this kind of a relationship are "because," "for," "since," "on account of," and "as a result."

> You do not have (A), *because* you do not ask God (B). When you ask, you do not receive (A), *because* you ask with wrong motives, that you may spend what you get on your pleasures (B). (James 4:2–3)

What then? Shall we sin (A) *because* we are not under law but under grace (B)? By no means! (Rom. 6:15)

Therefore, my dear friends, as you have always obeyed—not only in my presence, but now much more in my absence—continue to work out your salvation with fear and trembling (A), *for* it is God who works in you to will and to act according to his good purpose (B). (Phil. 2:12–13)

We have discussed in the previous section that the Greek term translated "work out" does not refer to earning or meriting and thus cannot refer to achieving salvation through works. This is revealed even more clearly by the causal relationship of Philippians 2:13 with what has preceded. It is *because* God is already at work in the lives of the Philippian Christians, *because* they are already the recipients of God's grace and salvation, that the exhortation is given to "work out" this salvation they possess. "Working out" their salvation is based on the fact that they already possess this salvation from God. For other examples, see Romans 11:20 ("because" introduces the cause), 30 ("as a result" introduces the cause); 12:1 ("in view of" introduces the cause); 1 Corinthians 1:21 ("For since" introduces the cause); 2 Corinthians 2:7 ("for" introduces the cause), 13 ("because" introduces the cause); Galatians 6:12 ("for" introduces the cause); 1 Thessalonians 5:8 ("since" introduces the cause).

2. Result—In this relationship (B) is the result of (A): "The man was wounded (A), *so that* he died (B)." Some of the terms used to describe this kind of a relationship are "so that," "that," "as a result," "therefore," and "so as to."

If I have the gift of prophecy and can fathom all mysteries and all knowledge, and if I have a faith (A) *that* can move mountains (B), but have not love, I am nothing. (1 Cor. 13:2)

The Lord's message rang out from you not only in Macedonia and Achaia—your faith in God has become known everywhere (A). *Therefore* we do not need to say anything about it (B). (1 Thess. 1:8)

And this is my prayer: that your love may abound more and more in knowledge and depth of insight (A), *so that* you may be able to discern what is best and may be pure and blameless until the day of Christ (B). (Phil. 1:9–10)

For other examples, see Romans 1:20 ("so that" expresses the result); 6:12 ("so that" expresses the result); 7:3 ("even though" expresses the result; cf. the NASB, which uses "so that"); 15:9 ("so that" expresses the result); Galatians 1:4 ("to" expresses the result); 2:13 ("so that" expresses the result); 3:17 ("and thus" expresses the result; cf. RSV and NASB, which use "so as to"); 5:17 ("so that" expresses the result).

3. Purpose—In this relationship (B) is the purpose of (A): "He allowed himself to be wounded (A) *in order that* he be sent home (B)." Purpose and result are quite similar, for if we are successful in what we have purposed, what results is the purpose. Purpose, however, refers to the intention of the action. Sometimes the distinction between purpose and result is both clear and important. The difference between manslaughter and first-degree murder is not the result but the intention. Shooting someone accidently or intentionally may have a similar result, the death of the victim, but the law recognizes that they are to be treated differently. This is true in the Old Testament, which permitted cities of refuge (Num. 35) for those whose actions resulted in killing someone but who did not purpose to do so. Some of the terms used to describe this kind of relationship are "in order that," "so that," "that," "to" plus an infinitive, "lest," and "rather."

I long to see you (A) *so that* I may impart to you some spiritual gift *to make* you strong (B). (Rom. 1:11)

Now we know that whatever the law says, it says to those who are under the law (A), *so that* every mouth may be silenced and the whole world held accountable to God (B). (Rom. 3:19)

All Scripture is God-breathed and is useful for teaching, rebuking, correcting and training in righteousness (A), *so that* the man of God may be thoroughly equipped for every good work (B). (2 Tim. 3:16–17)

For other examples, see Romans 7:4 ("that" expresses the purpose); 2 Corinthians 8:9 ("so that" expresses the purpose); 1 Corinthians 9:12 ("rather," i.e, "in order not to," expresses the purpose); 11:34 ("so that" expresses the purpose); Galatians 1:4 ("to" expresses the purpose); 6:12 (RSV "only in order" expresses the purpose); Philippians 3:10 (cf. RSV, NASB "that" expresses the purpose); 1 Thessalonians 3:5 ("to find out" expresses the purpose); 1 Timothy 4:15 ("so that" expresses the purpose).

4. Condition—(A) is the condition of (B): "*If* he was wounded (A), he would have been sent to the field hospital (B)." Some of the terms

used to describe this kind of relationship are "if," "if . . . then," "except,"and "unless."

> You, however, are controlled not by the sinful nature but by the Spirit (B), *if* the Spirit of God lives in you (A). *If* anyone does not have the Spirit of Christ (A), he does not belong to Christ (B). (Rom. 8:9)

> Therefore, *if* anyone is in Christ (A), he is a new creation (B); the old has gone, the new has come. (2 Cor. 5:17)

For other examples, see Romans 8:13 ("if" expresses the condition); 11:12 ("if" expresses the condition); 11:21 ("if" expresses the condition); 1 Corinthians 7:11 ("if" expresses the condition); 13:1 ("if" expresses the condition); Galatians 5:25 ("Since" expresses the condition; cf. the RSV, NASB, which use "if"); Colossians 2:20 ("Since" expresses the condition; cf. the RSV, NASB, which use "if").

   5. Concession—Despite (A), (B) took place: "*Even though* he was wounded (A), he did not die (B)." Some of the terms used to describe this kind of relationship are "despite," "even though," "although," "though," "yet," "apart," and "even if."

> *Even if* I caused you sorrow by my letter (A), I do not regret it (B). (2 Cor. 7:8)

> But *even if* we or an angel from heaven should preach a gospel other than the one we preached to you (A), let him be eternally condemned (B)! (Gal. 1:8)

> Have this mind among yourselves, which is yours in Christ Jesus, who, *though* he was in the form of God (A), did not count equality with God a thing to be grasped. . . (B). (Phil. 2:5–6 RSV)

For other examples, see Romans 3:21 ("apart" expresses concession); 5:10 ("if, when" expresses concession); Galatians 6:1 ("if someone" expresses concession); Philippians 2:17 ("But even if" expresses concession); Hebrews 5:8 ("Although" expresses concession), 12 ("though" expresses concession); 1 Peter 1:6 ("though" expresses concession).

   6. Means—(A) is the means by which (B) is accomplished: "*By* helicopter (A) the wounded were brought quickly to the field hospital (B)." Some of the terms used to describe this kind of relationship are "by," "with," "by means of," "through," and "in."

> For it is by grace you have been saved (B), *through* faith (A)—and this not from yourselves, it is the gift of God—not by works, so that no one can boast. (Eph. 2:8–9)

> For you know that it was not *with* perishable things such as silver or gold (A) that you were redeemed from the empty way of life handed down to you from your forefathers (B), but *with* the precious blood of Christ (A), a lamb without blemish or defect. (1 Pet. 1:18–19)

It is easy to confuse "means" and "cause." In the examples given above it should be noted that the wounded man was not brought to the field hospital *because* of a helicopter but by *means* of a helicopter. The cause for being brought to the field hospital was his wounds. Similarly, in Ephesians 2:8–9 the believer is not saved *because* of faith. Faith is not the "cause" but the "means" of salvation. All the faith in the world could not save a person if Jesus had not died for the sins of the world! The cause of salvation is God's grace in Christ, *by* grace (in Greek this is an instrumental of cause). The means through which this salvation is appropriated is *through* faith. The purpose (*so that*) is that no one should be able to boast before God. (If a person is saved from a life-threatening disease by means of an antibiotic, that person is saved *because* of the antibiotic that was administered by *means* of a hypodermic syringe. A person could be stuck day and night with the syringe, however, and become no better. It is not the syringe but the antibiotic that is the cause of the healing. The syringe is the means.)

For other examples, see Romans 12:2 ("by" expresses means); 1 Corinthians 2:13 ("in" expresses means); James 2:18 ("by" expresses means); 1 John 2:3 (cf. RSV "by this" expresses means).

7. Manner—(A) is done in the manner of (B): "He served his country (A) *by* enduring numerous wounds (B)." Some of the terms used to describe this kind of relationship are "by," "with," "by means of," and "from."

> If I take part in the meal (A) *with* thankfulness (B), why am I denounced because of something I thank God for? (1 Cor. 10:30)

> because our gospel came to you (A) not simply *with* words (B) but also *with* power (B) *with* the Holy Spirit (B) and *with* deep conviction (B). (1 Thess. 1:5)

> For the Lord himself will come down from heaven (A), *with* a loud command (B), with the voice of an archangel (B) and *with* the trumpet call of God (B), and the dead in Christ will rise first. (1 Thess. 4:16)

For other examples, see 1 Corinthians 9:26 ("aimlessly" and "beating the air" express manner); 11:5 ("with" expresses manner); Galatians 6:11 (cf. RSV "with" expresses manner); Philippians 1:18 ("from" expresses manner; cf. RSV "in").

There are other kinds of relationships that clauses and phrases can have, but these seem to be the most important. It should be observed that in the norms of language the same word can introduce a number of different relationships. For instance, "so that" can be used to introduce purpose or result; "by" can introduce cause, means, or manner. The specific relationship is decided by the meaning the author has willed through the surrounding context. It is from the context that the range of possibilities permitted by the norms of language can be narrowed down to the one specific meaning intended by the author. This is true not only in the original Greek and Hebrew text in which the author has expressed his meaning, but also in the English version being used. Here also the authors reveal how they want their readers to interpret the relationship of their clauses and phrases by means of the literary context they give. To understand the reasoning of the biblical authors, we must pay careful attention to how they related the clauses and phrases they have written. This is true not only of the Epistles but of all parts of the Bible. It is especially important, however, with respect to the Epistles because it is within this literary form that we encounter the most carefully reasoned arguments found in the Bible.

Conclusion

In seeking to interpret the Epistles, the person able to study the Bible in its original languages possesses two distinct advantages over the person studying the Bible in translation. One is that there are certain grammatical insights that can be gleaned from the author's writings that are not available to the person who must read them in translation. For instance, at times the tense of the Greek verb, which cannot be easily conveyed into an English translation, is quite significant. In Romans 12:2 Paul's use of the present imperative of prohibition indicates that he is not telling the Romans "Don't allow yourselves to become conformed to this world . . ." but rather "Stop allowing yourselves to be conformed to this world." The implication of this in preaching should not be missed. If the Roman Christians, without the kind of media barrage that we experience today, were unconsciously allowing their values and thinking to be shaped by this present world and the god of this age, it is even more likely that this is happening to us today. We need to be aware of this and stop permitting this to continue.

Knowing that the tense of the verb in 1 John 3:9 ("will continue" and "cannot go on sinning") is a present tense also helps in translating this difficult verse. Since the present tense, more often than not, gives the sense of continual action, this helps us to understand that John is not saying that the Christian never sins, which would contradict what he has already said in 1 John 1:9–2:2, but that the Christian does not continually abide in sin. The New International Version has translated this in a helpful way, but the King James–Revised Standard Version tradition unfortunately confuses the reader. Even as in the teaching of Chinese or French literature the teacher who possesses facility in these languages has an advantage over the one who does not, so the student of the Bible who has facility in the biblical languages has an advantage over the one who does not.

The second advantage of knowing the biblical languages involves a difference in the goal of interpretation. Whereas the interpreter of Romans who has facility in Greek can seek as his or her goal the discovery of Paul's meaning, the reader of a translation cannot. The goal of reading a translation of the Bible is to understand the meaning of the translators. This can be demonstrated rather simply. If we do not understand a word in an English translation, where do we look? In a contemporary English dictionary, of course. But Paul did not know English! Thus, we are not looking at what Paul meant by this English word but what the translators meant. A reader of the Bible in translation is a step removed from the meaning of the biblical writer, whereas those who have facility in the original languages have direct access to the text of the author.

Having said this, it should be pointed out that the translators of such versions as the New International Version, the Revised Standard Version, and the New English Bible possessed a remarkable grasp of the languages of the Bible and the meaning of its authors. In addition, they possessed a facility as well for expressing, interpreting, their understanding of the biblical authors. Thus, we can have great confidence in the translations we are reading. Their accuracy is remarkable, and of all the countries of the world we are most blessed with numerous, highly accurate translations. In my study I have nearly two dozen such translations. In those instances in which we are carefully studying a particular text or passage, it is advantageous to compare several translations.

Questions

1. Why would a departure by Paul from the normal epistolary form be more significant than his following it?

2. Why would understanding the meaning of various words in the Greek Old Testament (LXX) be more helpful in studying Paul's use of these words than understanding the meaning of these words in classical Greek or modern Greek writers?

3. Look up two or three references in each section of 3 a–g and observe how the context given by the authors helps in understanding the grammatical relationship between the clauses.

4. What is the advantage of knowing Greek and Hebrew in the study of the Bible?

5. Where can a person who does not know the biblical languages go to find assistance in interpreting the Bible?

13

The Games
of Treaties, Laws, and Songs

In this final chapter we shall look at three additional literary forms found in the Bible. There are, of course, many other forms that could be discussed. The selection of the forms discussed in this book is somewhat arbitrary, but they represent those most frequently found in the Bible. Some have not been discussed because the rules that apply to them are dealt with elsewhere. Thus, such forms as similes and metaphors are not discussed because the principles described in the chapter on parables are applicable to them. Similarly, we have not treated the Gospels as a separate literary type, because they can be included in the larger category of biblical narrative. We have likewise treated apocalyptic literature in the chapter on prophecy. We shall not discuss such forms as riddles, satire, visions, midrash, household codes, genealogies, the supposed "we" travel narrative form (which we now know never existed), or theophanies because of the limitations of space.

Two of the forms we shall study, covenant and law, are closely related, for the laws of the Bible assume a covenantal relationship between God and the believer. The final form we shall look at involves the various kinds of psalms.

Covenant

The importance of the covenant in the Bible is not always recognized. We read of the covenants God made with Adam/Eve and Noah.

It is, however, the Abrahamic covenant that is the most important. This covenant (Gen. 12, 15, 17) is renewed with Isaac (Gen. 26:1–5) and Jacob (Gen. 28:10–17; 35:9–15), remembered (Exod. 2:23–25) and renewed (Exod. 19:1–9; Deut. 7:6–11) during the exodus from Egypt, renewed with Joshua (Josh. 24:14–27, esp. vv. 25–27), and referred to time and time again in the Old Testament (with David—2 Sam. 7:8–15; 23:5; by Solomon—1 Kings 8:9, 23; by the biblical narrator—2 Kings 13:23; etc.). A new covenant is referred to in Jeremiah 31:31–34, which finds its fulfillment in Jesus (Luke 22:20; 1 Cor. 11:25). And it is this new covenant, initiated with Abraham, which is the hope of the believer (Acts 3:25; Gal. 3:6–9, 15–18, 29).

A great deal has been learned in the past century concerning the covenant form. This is due to the discovery of numerous such covenants in the literature of the ancient Near East, especially in the Hittite literature. There were two main kinds of covenants. The difference between them depends on the relationship of the people involved. If the relationship involves equals (1 Sam. 18:3; 1 Kings 5:12), this results in a "parity" covenant. In such a covenant both parties mutually agree as equals to obey identical stipulations. The other form is called a "suzerain" covenant. This is not a treaty among equals, for an ancient suzerain was a feudal lord. In a suzerain covenant the lord unilaterally established the terms and conditions for his subjects. The subjects in turn could only accept or reject the covenant and its terms. This kind of covenant contained such things as:

- Preamble—In the preamble the author of the covenant identifies himself.

- Historical Prologue—This describes the previous relationship of the two parties and emphasizes the gracious character of the suzerain in his past dealings with the lesser party. It provides justification for the following stipulations.

- Stipulations—This describes the obligations and responsibilities of the lesser party and involves such things as prohibition of establishing relationships and treaties with other nations (cf. "You shall have no other gods before me," Exod. 20:3); support for the suzerain; obligation to hate the enemies of the suzerain; various prohibitions and commands; and the like. These stipulations are not conditions for entering the covenant but for remaining true to it. The prime stipulation involves loyalty to the suzerain.

- Provision for Continual Reading—This was meant to insure familiarity with the covenant by the people and their descendants.

- List of Witnesses—Frequently the suzerain would appeal to the gods (cf. in the Old Testament "heaven and earth") to bear witness to the establishment of the covenant.
- Blessings and Cursings—These are contingent on the obedience or disobedience of the subjects.
- Oath—The subjects here pledge obedience to the covenant and to its stipulations.

All these elements are not always present. The most important are the preamble, the historical dialogue, the stipulations, and the blessings and cursings.

Biblical Covenant	Declarations of Covenants, Conditions, and Restrictions

Preamble
———
———
Historical Prologue
———
Stipulations
———
Cursings and Blessings
———
List of Witnesses
———
Provision for Continual Reading
———
Oath
———
	———
	———
	Witnessed
	———
	Definitions
	  1. Party A
	  2. Party B
	Duties of Party A
	  1. Security
	  2. Landscaping
	  3. Collection and Garbage
	———
	Duties of Party B
	  1. Maintenance and Repair
	  2. Minimum Landscape Plan
	  3. Mailboxes
	———

Within the Old Testament no divine covenant follows the order listed above exactly or contains all these elements, but it is evident that the Old Testament covenants are patterned along similar lines. The Abrahamic covenant, and the other versions of this covenant, are clearly not "parity" covenants. They are not covenants among equals. On the contrary, the conditions of the covenant are made unilaterally. It is the LORD God of Israel who graciously establishes these covenants and who determines their conditions. The covenant established with the people of Israel, however, is gracious. It is not earned or merited but due entirely to the mercy and kindness of God. Even the blessings are not earned or merited, for they are offered as rewards for obedience, not as pay earned!

When we compare the Old Testament covenants with the form of the suzerain covenant, we find some remarkable parallels:

Genesis 12:1–3

Preamble—"The LORD had said to Abram . . ." (v. 1)

Stipulations—"Leave your country, your people and your father's household and go to the land I will show you." (v. 1)

Blessings—"I will make you into a great nation and I will bless you." (v. 2)

Genesis 17:1–14

Preamble—"I am God almighty." (v. 1)

Stipulations—"This is my covenant. . . . Every male among you will be circumcised . . ." (vv. 10–14)

Blessings—"I will confirm my covenant . . . and will greatly increase your numbers." (v. 2) "You will be the father of many nations . . ." (vv. 4–8, 15–16)

Exodus 19–24

Preamble—"I am the LORD your God . . ." (20:1)

Historical Prologue—"This is what you are to say to the house of Jacob and what you are to tell the people of Israel: 'You yourselves have seen what I did to Egypt, and how I carried you on eagles' wings and brought you to myself.'" (19:3–4) "I am the LORD your God, who brought you out of Egypt, out of the land of slavery." (20:2)

Stipulations—"Now if you obey me fully and keep my covenant." (19:5) "You shall have no other gods before me . . ." (20:3–17)

Provision for Continual Reading—"Then he took the Book of the Covenant and read it to the people." (24:7)

List of Witnesses—"The people all responded together . . ." (19:8; 24:3, 7)

Oath—"'We will do everything the LORD has said.'" (19:8) "When Moses went and told the people all the LORD's words and laws, they responded with one voice, 'Everything the LORD has said we will do.'" (24:3)

Deuteronomy

Preamble—"These are the word Moses spoke to all Israel . . ." (1:1–5)

Historical Prologue—This involves 1:6–4:49.

Stipulations—This goes from 5:1 to 26:19 and includes general (5:1–11:32) and specific commands (12:1–26:19).

Cursings and Blessings—These are found in 27:1–30:20.

List of Witnesses—"This day I call heaven and earth as witnesses against you . . ." (30:19; 31:19; 32:1; cf. also 4:26)

Provision for Continual Reading—We find this in 27:1–14; 31:9–13.

Joshua 24:1–33

Preamble—"Joshua said to all the people . . ." (vv. 1–2a)

Historical Prologue—"Long ago your forefathers . . . lived beyond the River and worshiped other gods. But I took your father Abraham from the land beyond the River and led him . . ." (vv. 2b–13)

Stipulations—"Now fear the LORD and serve him . . ." (vv. 14–21)

List of Witnesses—"'You are witnesses against yourselves that you have chosen to serve the Lord.' 'Yes, we are witnesses,' they replied." (v. 22)

Provision for Continual Reading—"And Joshua recorded these things in the Book of the Law of God." (v. 26)

Oath—"On that day Joshua made a covenant for the people, and there at Shechem he drew up for them decrees and laws." (v. 25)

The parallels between the examples given above and ancient suzerain treaties are quite impressive. The writers of Scripture as they recorded these covenants expected their readers to recognize them as "suzerain" treaties and to understand their various elements. Knowing this treaty form and what is involved enables us to interpret the biblical examples better. We shall mention two principles involved in the interpretation of such treaty forms.

For one, the unilateral and gracious nature of the biblical covenants must be kept in mind. These covenants are not treaties among equals. On the contrary, they originated in the graciousness of a most superior "party"—God himself! Thus, at the start we must remember that they should not be interpreted as a means of placing God in our debt or under obligation to us. The sovereign Lord may willingly obligate himself to us, but this has nothing to do with our worthiness or merit. The covenant originated in grace and is based on grace alone.

Second, the stipulations found in a covenant are not to be understood as requirements in order to initiate a positive relationship with God. On the contrary, they presume an already existing covenantal relationship. The ten commandments of Exodus 20:2–17 are not directed to people outside a covenantal relationship, revealing how they may enter into such a relationship. They are given to God's people who have already been "redeemed" from bondage (Exod. 20:1) and describe how that relationship can be maintained and how continued divine blessing may be experienced.

Law and Commandments

In the Bible a large section, the books of Genesis through Deuteronomy, is called the "Law." The "Law" can also refer to the entire Old Testament (cf. John 10:34; 12:34; 15:25; 1 Cor. 14:21, which refer to the "Law" but quote another part of the Old Testament). Usually, however, the Law is associated with Exodus 20–Deuteronomy 33. Within this section we find material other than laws. However, since there are over six hundred commandments or laws found in Genesis–Deuteronomy, these five books are usually referred to as "The Law." (Genesis does not contain any of this legal material but is part of the Law, because it serves as the introduction to Exodus–Deuteronomy and because it was assumed that Moses wrote all these books. In actuality, however, most of these five books, called the "Pentateuch," consists of narrative.)

When we compare the laws found in this section of the Old Testament with ancient Near Eastern laws, we can observe at times a striking similarity. For instance, the laws concerning false witness (Exod.

23:1–3; Deut. 19:16–21; cf. Hammurabi Laws 1, 3, 4), kidnapping (Exod. 21:16; cf. Hammurabi Laws 14), animals left to the safekeeping of others (Exod. 22:10–13; cf. Hammurabi Laws 266–67), animals borrowed from others (Exod. 22:14–15; cf. Hittite Laws 75), an ox goring another ox (Exod. 21:35–36; cf. Eshnunna Laws 53–54; Hammurabi Laws 250–51) are alike in both content and wording with laws and regulations in other societies of the ancient Near East. Note the following example:

> If a seignior [a man of rank] has destroyed the eye of the son of a man [of similar rank], they shall destroy his eye. (Hammurabi Laws 196)

> If any one injures his neighbor, whatever he has done must be done to him: fracture for fracture, eye for eye, tooth for tooth. As he has injured the other, so he is to be injured. (Lev. 24:19–20)

The laws of the Bible have been classified according to their form into two types: casuistic law and apodictic law. The former is a case-by-case law, which usually goes something like "*If* A takes place, *then* B will be the consequences." Casuistic law usually involves secular or civil matters. Apodictic law, however, is declarative and categorical. It tends to consist of prohibitions, commands, and instructions. These laws are often unqualified and tend to be more "religious" in nature. Most laws in the ancient Near East tend to be casuistic. This is also true with respect to the Old Testament.

The laws of the Bible are not exhaustive in nature. They serve as patterns that govern behavior by means of the implications contained within those patterns of meaning. Thus the command "You shall not commit adultery" (Exod. 20:14) has numerous implications concerning lust (cf. Matt. 5:27–30) and pornography even though these things are not explicitly mentioned in the command itself. Perhaps a useful analogy between the laws contained in the Old Testament and their various implications is how the Constitution of the United States relates to the various laws passed by Congress. The articles of the Constitution contain implications that these laws bring out. (The analogy is not a perfect one, however, because some laws passed by Congress may violate the Constitution. Others may not be contained within the pattern of meaning of the Constitution but do not violate them.) The laws of the Old Testament were understood by their author(s) as involving patterns of meaning that went beyond the specific meaning found in the law itself, even as the authors of the Constitution understood their work as containing numerous unstated implications.

Another distinction frequently made between various laws involves not so much their form as their content. These are frequently divided into three classifications: ethical laws (such as the Ten Commandments or Ten "Words" [Exod. 20:1; 34:27–28; Deut. 4:13; 10:4]); cultic laws (such as the ritual laws involving sacrifices, qualifications for priestly duty, prohibition of unclean foods, etc.); and civil laws (penalties for crimes, inheritance regulations, etc.). Some have objected to this three-fold division because the Old Testament does not explicitly make such a distinction and at times these classifications appear to overlap. Were the laws regulating disease and cleansing (Lev. 13–15) cultic or civil? Were they both? Because they involve priests and sacrifice, it is not easy to determine.

The distinction among the ethical, cultic, and civil dimensions of the law, however, is both useful and grounded in the New Testament distinction. Jesus saw a distinction between the cultic and ethical dimensions of the law when he said, "Nothing outside a man can make him 'unclean' by going into him. Rather, it is what comes out of a man that makes him 'unclean'" (Mark 7:14; cf. also vv. 18–23). Mark also understood the distinction when he added the comment "(In saying this, Jesus declared all food 'clean.')" (Mark 7:19). Luke and Paul likewise witness to this distinction in Acts 10; 15; Galatians 2:11–21; 1 Corinthians 6:12–20; 8; 10:23–11:1; and above all Romans 14.

When the New Testament refers to the laws of the Old Testament, it understands the cultic and civil laws as being no longer binding. The Old Testament foresaw that a time would come when a new covenant would be established. At that time some of the stipulations involved in the old covenant would come to an end. In the new covenant all foods are cleansed (Mark 7:19; cf. Acts 10:9–16), the sacrificial system and its priesthood have been made superfluous through the once-for-all sacrifice of Jesus and his eternal priesthood on our behalf (Heb. 7–8; 10:1–10), and circumcision is no longer required (Gal. 5:2–6). The civil laws of the Old Testament are also no longer binding since biblical Israel no longer exists. The principles of such laws, however, may still reflect divine guidelines that an organized society would do well to follow. Such principles, which limit revenge and seek reciprocity between crime and punishment ("eye for eye, tooth for tooth, hand for hand, foot for foot, burn for burn, wound for wound, bruise for bruise,"

Exod. 21:24–25) and which see a difference in actions according to whether they are intentional or accidental (Num. 35:6–34), provide good counsel for any society to follow.

As to the ethical dimension of the Old Testament laws, there is no reason to think that they would change drastically, for they reflect the character of God. The New Testament writers understand them as still binding. Certainly Matthew understands them in this way when he quotes Jesus, "Do not think that I have come to abolish the Law of the Prophets; I have not come to abolish them but to fulfill them. . . . Anyone who breaks one of the least of these commandments and teaches others to do the same will be called least in the kingdom of heaven, but whoever practices and teaches these commands will be called great in the kingdom of heaven" (Matt. 5:17–20). Matthew then proceeds to show that the greater righteousness that Jesus demands involves not merely an external keeping of the specific commands of the law. The Pharisees and teachers of the law did that. In Matthew 5:21–48 the higher righteousness Jesus demanded involves keeping the entire pattern of meaning found in these commands and their various implications. Jesus' summary of the whole law as encapsulated in the two commands to love God and one's neighbor (Mark 12:28–34) also indicates that the ethical teachings of the law are still to be kept. The fact that Paul (Gal. 5:14; Rom. 13:9) and James (James 2:8) quote Jesus' summary of the law indicate that they thought similarly. It is best therefore to assume that these Old Testament laws are still binding for the believer unless specifically abrogated in the New Testament.

In interpreting the laws of the Bible it is important to remember several things. First of all, we must remember that they are associated with a covenant of grace. The attempt to keep the commandments perfectly will always fail and can never lead to salvation. Due to our fallen nature and sin, we do not and cannot keep the commandments (Rom. 3:1–20). Furthermore, the attempt to keep the commandments cannot save, because to be saved one must be a beneficiary of the covenant of grace. Yet it is only after a covenantal relationship is already established based on God's grace that the stipulations of the law are given. We must never forget how covenant and law are related. It is after God establishes a covenant of grace with his people that the stipulations of the law are given. The exodus (Exod. 14; 20:2) preceded the giving of the law on Mount Sinai (Exod. 20:3–17)! The order cannot be reversed! Salvation precedes obedience.

Yet after a person has entered into this covenant and has become God's servant, he or she needs to and desires to serve God. The new nature and heart-felt gratitude of the believer demand this. The recent debate on lordship-salvation or "Once saved—always saved?" has all too often lost sight of the fact that salvation takes place within a covenantal relationship. That covenant brings with it numerous benefits. One of them is regeneration. The regenerated heart and will seek to serve God. What serving God involves is described in the laws or stipulations he has given in his covenant. How that service is then rendered is by obedience to those laws. It would be a strange "faith" indeed that did not result in a regenerated heart and life and that was unconcerned or antagonistic toward God's laws. However else the Bible might describe such a "faith," it would not describe it as "saving faith." It is more like the faith James describes as possessed by demons (James 2:19).

Another principle for interpreting the laws of the Bible is to note that their specific meaning does not exhaust all their meaning. The laws of the Bible are patterns of meaning that contain numerous implications. Even if the law is worded as a specific command or prohibition rather than a general principle, its meaning is not exhausted by obeying the specific law. Thus, even laws that seem out-of-date and no longer applicable may carry useful and appropriate implications for today. If a command such as "eye for eye, tooth for tooth" does not seem to be applicable today, it is only because the interpreter is not aware of the pattern of meaning and the various implications contained in that statement. Its principle, that punishment should fit the crime, will always be relevant.

Similarly, the casuistic law found in Exodus 21:28–29 has important implications for today: "If a bull gores a man or a woman to death, the bull must be stoned to death, and its meat must not be eaten. But the owner of the bull will not be held responsible. If, however, the bull has had the habit of goring and the owner has been warned but has not kept it penned up and it kills a man or woman, the bull must be stoned and the owner also must be put to death." In practice this penalty does not seem to have been literally carried out in Israel, but a severe financial penalty was administered. Today, too, we need to make a distinction between harm or death brought about by accident or through careless negligence.

One additional principle for interpreting the laws of the Bible can be mentioned. The law has as one of its purposes the revelation of our sin and depravity. Even in our best moments we fail to keep the laws of

God perfectly. Thus, we must recognize that we need forgiveness and grace. The law seeks to show us our need of God's grace. If we stand outside a covenantal relationship with God, it drives us to repent and seek God's saving grace. If we stand within that covenantal relationship, it shows us that time and time again we fail to keep the divine stipulations of the covenant and that we must confess our sins (1 John 1:9) and pray, "Forgive us our debts" (Matt. 6:12). We enter into a covenantal relationship with God on the basis of grace alone, and that relationship is maintained on the basis of grace as well.

Psalms

Psalms is by far the largest book in the Bible. It consists of 150 individual psalms arranged in five "Books." Each Book (1–41; 42–72; 73–89; 90–106; 107–150) ends with a doxology (41:13; 72:18–19; 89:52; 106:48; and 150, which serves as a doxology for the last book and the Psalms as a whole). The Psalms and its present arrangement were compiled over a period of time. This is clear from the editorial comment found in 72:20, "This concludes the prayers of David son of Jesse." The largest number of psalms are attributed to David (73), but others are attributed to Asaph (12), the Sons of Korah (11), Solomon (2), and Moses (1). Some of the psalms are even repeated in part or as a whole (14 = 53; 40:13–17 = 70; 57:7–11 = 108:1–5; 60:5–12 = 108:6–13). (Some other places where psalms can be found are Exod. 15:1–18; Deut. 32:1–43; 1 Sam. 2:1–10; 2 Sam. 22:2–51; Isa. 12:4–6; Jonah 2:2–10; Hab. 3:2–19; etc.)

We have dealt with the rhythmic nature of the psalms in the chapter on poetry. Here we shall deal with the forms of the psalms themselves rather than the kinds of poetry found within them. These forms are not rigid and some of the classifications are somewhat arbitrary.

Psalms of Lament

These make up the largest number of psalms. They consist of both individual lament (3–7, 13, 17, 22, 25–28, 31, 35, 39, 42–43, 51, 54–57, 59, 61–64, 70–71, 77, 86, 88, 102, 120, 130, 140–43) and national lament psalms (44, 74, 79–80, 83, 85, 90, 94, 137). The exact number is uncertain because the classification of certain psalms is debated. Although not all the following elements are contained in each, we frequently find:

- Address to God—"O LORD" (13:1); "O God" (74:1); "to the Lord" (142:1). Sometimes the reason why an appeal is made to this God is included, as in "O LORD my God" (7:1); "O Shepherd of Israel, you who lead Joseph like a flock; you who sit enthroned" (80:1); "O LORD, the God who saves me" (88:1; cf. also 5:2; 70:1, 79:9).

- Lament or Description of Need—"Will you forget me forever? How long will you hide your face from me? How long must I wrestle with my thoughts and every day have sorrow in my heart? How long will my enemy triumph over me?" (13:1–2); "Have you rejected us forever . . . Why does your anger smolder against the sheep of your pasture . . ." (74:1–11); "day and night I cry out before you . . ." (88:1b–12); "I cry aloud. . . ." (142:1–4). At times within the lament there is found a protest or claim of innocence by the Psalmist (7:3–5, 8–9; 17:3–5; 26:1–3; etc.).

- Petition or Prayer for Help—"Look on me and answer, O LORD my God" (13:3–4); "Remember how the enemy has mocked you, O LORD, how foolish people have reviled your name . . ." (74:18–23); "But I cry to you for help, O LORD; in the morning my prayer comes before you . . ." (88:13–18); "I cry to you, O LORD; I say, 'You are my refuge, my portion in the land of the living.' Listen to my cry . . ." (142:5a, 6). Usually the petition involves help and rescue in the present life, but in 49:15 and 73:24 the divine salvation involves the life to come.

- Confession of Confidence—"But I trust in your unfailing love; my heart rejoices in your salvation" (13:5); "But you, O God, are my king from of old; you bring salvation upon the earth. It was you who split open the sea by your power . . ." (74:12–17); (this is missing in Psalm 88); "I say, 'You are my refuge, my portion in the land of the living.'" (142:5b–c, 7c–d).

- Vow or Confession of Praise—"I will sing to the Lord, for he has been good to me" (13:6); (missing in Psalms 74 and 88); "Set me free from my prison, that I may praise your name" (142:7a–b); "From the LORD comes deliverance. May your blessing be on your people" (3:8); "I will give thanks to the LORD because of his righteousness and will sing praise to the name of the LORD Most High" (7:17).

Psalms of Praise and Thanksgiving

These psalms are the opposite of the lament psalms. Although some have sought to make these into two different kinds of psalms (praise psalms and thanksgiving psalms), they are probably best seen as one and the same. Both thanksgiving and praise go together. There is no thanksgiving without praise and no praise without thanksgiving. As in the psalms of lament, we have individual (8, 18, 30, 32–34, 40, 66, 75, 81, 92, 103–4, 106, 108, 111–13, 116, 118, 135, 138, 145–50) and group (65, 67, 107, 114, 117, 124, 136) praise and thanksgiving psalms. At times it is difficult to know whether a psalm is better classified as an individual or group praise psalm (cf. 145–150). This form of psalm generally contains the following:

- Introductory Praise—Frequently they begin with a call to: "Praise the LORD (Hallelujah)" (106:1; 111:1; 112:1; 113:1; 135:1; 146:1; 147:1; 148:1; 149:1; 150:1); "Bless the LORD, O my soul (RSV—103:1; 104:1; cf. also 34:1; 67:1; 134:1; 145:1); "I will praise you, O LORD, with all my heart" (138:1). Sometimes the introductory call of praise is directed to a person or group: "Praise the LORD, O my soul; all my inmost being, praise his holy name" (103:1b–2; 146:1b–2); "Let Israel rejoice in their Maker; let the people of Zion be glad in their King" (149:2); "My soul will boast in the LORD; let the afflicted hear and rejoice" (34:2); "Shout with joy to God, all the earth" (66:1). There may even be a call to a particular mode of praise: "Let them praise his name with dancing and make music to him with tambourine and harp" (149:3; cf. also 33:2–3; 81:2–3; 92:3; 108:2; 147:7; 150:3–5).

- Description of What God Has Done—This may involve God's deliverance from persecution, illness, or forgiveness of sins. "Who forgives all your sins and heals all your diseases, who redeems your life from the pit. . . . " (103:3–19); "When I called, you answered me; you made me bold and stouthearted . . ." (138:3–7); "Do not put your trust in princes. . . . Blessed is he whose help is the God of Jacob. . . . He upholds the cause of the oppressed . . ." (146:3–9); "For the LORD takes delight in his people; he crowns the humble with salvation . . . ." (149:4–9).

- Concluding Word or Call to Praise—Although some psalms lack this, others conclude with "Praise the LORD" [Hallelujah] (104:35; 116:19; 117:2). Some even begin and conclude this way (106:1, 48; 113:1, 9; 135:1, 21; 146:1, 10; 148:1, 14; 149:1, 9; 150:1, 6; cf. also 8:1, 9; 103:1, 22; 104:1, 35; 118:1, 29). Others conclude: "O LORD my God, I will give you thanks forever" (30:12); "Rejoice in the LORD and be glad you righteous; sing, all you who are upright in heart" (32:11); "Praise be to God, who has not rejected my prayer or withheld his love from me!" (66:20).

Several other kinds of psalms, whose classification is due less to form than to content, can also be mentioned.

- Psalms of Zion—These do not possess a specific form but their content frequently centers on Jerusalem and the temple. Some examples of this are: 46, 48, 76, 84, 87, 122; cf. also 137.
- Royal Psalms—These are frequently associated with the messianic hope, because the pattern of the good king in these psalms ultimately describe "the" anointed king who is to come, the Messiah (2, 18, 20–21, 45, 72, 89, 101, 110, 132, 144).
- Hymns to God—It is not easy to distinguish these from psalms of praise and thanksgiving, but these would include: 19, 24, 29, 47, 95–100, 104.
- Wisdom Psalms—These include such psalms as 1, 37, 49, 73, 112, 127–128, 133.
- Trust Psalms—This classification is somewhat arbitrary, but this theme is found in: 11, 16, 23, 62, 91, 121, 125, 131.
- Penitential Psalms—We have treated this form of psalm under the general category of psalms of lament. Those lament psalms which are frequently called "penitential" are: 6, 32, 38, 51, 102, 130.
- Imprecatory Psalms—We have referred briefly to these (35, 58, 69, 83, 109, 137) in the chapter on idioms. (See p. 130.)

Although knowledge of these forms is useful for classifying the psalms, the primary value lies in the area of interpretation. An example of this can be seen in Psalm 13. At the end of this lament psalm the confession of confidence and the vow of praise found in verses 5–6 look entirely out of place. There is no logical connection between these two verses and what has preceded. Yet they are not some later scribal addition to the psalm to make it more devout. On the contrary, they are normal elements in a lament psalm. They are vital parts in this literary form. Rather than appearing out of place, they should be expected by the reader. The psalmist in his lament is addressing his God. When he does so, he always has the goodness and mercy of God in mind. Thus, he "laments in hope" with the expectation that what God has promised in his covenant he will do on his behalf. We must always read such laments in light of the fact that they are not made in despair but in faith. The psalmist addressed God not in order to curse or condemn him but to remind him of his oath and covenant, in the hope that in doing so God would deliver him.

The faith manifested in a psalm of lament involves the essence of a person's relationship with God. The parallel between the form of such psalms and the order of worship found in many Christian churches should be noted:

Psalm of Lament	Church Service
Address to God	Call to Worship/Invocation
Lament or Description of Need	Prayer of Confession
Petition or Prayer for Help	Prayer of Confession
Confession of Confidence	Assurance of Forgiveness/Lord's Prayer
Vow or Confession of Praise	Concluding Hymn/Doxology

A thanksgiving or praise psalm reveals that the cause for such praise and thanksgiving always rests on what God has done in the past and the gracious covenant he has established. It is not based on philosophical truths or abstract attributes of God. Even God's future acts are based on what he has done in the past. This may involve those actions he has done on the part of the individual (some scholars refer to such thanksgiving psalms as "declarative praise psalms") or what he has done for the redeemed community (these are sometimes called "descriptive praise psalms"). Thus, we must remember that such psalms arise from the covenantal relationship the psalmist and his readers possess with God. There are some psalms that refer to God's greatness in creation (8:3–8; 19:1–6; 104). Yet even if the psalmist refers to this or God's providence over creation (65:6–13), he is referring not to the God of the nations, but to the God of Abraham, Isaac, and Jacob. It is the God who has chosen Israel, who is being praised.

Questions

1. What is a "covenant"? Do you belong to any covenant, such as a community covenant of homeowners? An organization that has a covenant?

2. How is the covenant God made with the children of Israel like a human covenant? How is it unlike a human covenant?

3. How are "law" and "covenant" related? Can you have only one?

4. Why are lament psalms not psalms of despair?

Glossary

application—The way meaning applies to the reader, i.e., significance; or implications that stem from the pattern of meaning.

author—The actual writer who penned the work being interpreted.

context—The author's willed meaning of the passages surrounding the text.

conviction—That work of the Holy Spirit that brings assurance of the truthfulness of the meaning of the Bible.

enlightenment—In biblical studies that period in history (primarily the nineteenth century) when the miracles of the Bible began to be doubted and denied.

exegesis—The process of understanding and interpreting a text.

generic expectation—The interpreting of a text, based upon a conclusion as to its literary form, using the rules governing that literary form.

genre—*See* literary genre.

implication—Those meanings in a text of which the author was unaware but which nevertheless legitimately fall with the pattern (or type) of meaning he or she willed.

intentional fallacy—An objection to seeking the willed meaning of the author because of the belief that a reader can never relive the experiences of the author when he wrote, i.e., their mental acts, or that author may not be able to express adequately their intended meaning.

interpretation—The verbal or written expression of one's understanding of a text's meaning.

illumination—The special guidance that the Holy Spirit supposedly gives to believers in understanding the meaning of the Bible.

langua—A French word that is a synonym for "norms of language."

literary genre—The literary form being used by the author and the rules governing that form.

meaning—The pattern of meaning the author willed to convey by the words (shareable symbols) he or she used.

mental acts—The experiences that the author went through when writing the text.

mental experiences—A synonym for mental acts.

norms of language—The possible range of meanings allowed by the words (verbal symbols) of a text.

norms of utterance—The specific meaning that the author has given to a word, phrase, sentence, etc. in a text.

parole—A French word that is a synonym for "norms of utterance."

pattern of meaning—The conscious willed meaning of the author and all its implications.

shareability—The common understanding of the language of the text possessed by both the author and his intended readers.

significance—How a reader responds to the meaning of a text.

subject matter—The content or "stuff" talked about in a text.

subtype—A synonym for "implication."

type—A synonym for "pattern of meaning."

unconscious meaning—A synonym for "implication."

Select Bibliography

Adler, Mortimer J. *How to Read a Book*. New York: Simon and Schuster, 1940.

Bailey, James L., and Lyle D. Vander Broek. *Literary Forms in the New Testament*. Louisville: Westminster/John Knox, 1992.

Caird, G. B. *The Language and Imagery of the Bible*. Philadelphia: Westminster, 1980.

Cotterell, Peter, and Max Turner. *Linguistics and Biblical Interpretation*. Downers Grove: InterVarsity, 1989.

Fee, Gordon D., and Douglas Stuart. *How to Read the Bible for All Its Worth*. 2d ed. Grand Rapids: Zondervan, 1982.

Hirsch, E. D., Jr. *Validity in Interpretation*. New Haven: Yale University Press, 1967.

Kaiser, Walter, and Moisés Silva. *An Introduction to Biblical Hermeneutics*. Grand Rapids: Zondervan, 1994.

Klein, William W., Craig L. Blomberg, and Robert L. Hubbard Jr. *Introduction to Biblical Interpretation*. Waco: Word, 1993.

Lewis, C.S. "Fern-seed and Elephants" in *Fern-seed and Elephants*. Glasgow: Fontana/Collins, 1975.

Osborne, Grant R. *The Hermeneutical Spiral*. Downers Grove: InterVarsity, 1991.

Ryken, Leland. *How to Read the Bible as Literature*. Grand Rapids: Zondervan, 1984.

Schreiner, Thomas R. *Interpreting the Pauline Epistles*. Grand Rapids: Baker, 1990.

Silva, Moisés. *Biblical Words and Their Meaning*. Grand Rapids: Zondervan, 1983.

Thiselton, Anthony C. *New Horizons in Hermeneutics*. Grand Rapids: Zondervan, 1992.

Virkler, Henry A. *Hermeneutics: Principles and Processes of Biblical Interpretation*. Grand Rapids: Baker, 1981.

Subject Index

Scripture Index